ONE HUNDRED YEARS AN ORPHAN

ST. VINCENT'S
San Francisco's Home for Boys
at San Rafael

1855 — 1955

by

JOHN T. DWYER

Priest of the Archdiocese of San Francisco

AN AUTHORS GUILD BACKINPRINT.COM EDITION

iUniverse, Inc.
Bloomington

One Hundred Years an Orphan
St. Vincent's, San Francisco's Home for Boys in San Rafael, 1855-1955

AN AUTHORS GUILD BACKINPRINT.COM EDITION

Published by iUniverse, Inc.

For information address:
iUniverse
1663 Liberty Drive
Bloomington, IN 47403
www.iuniverse.com
1-800-Authors (1-800-288-4677)

Originally published by Academy Library Guild

ISBN: 978-1-4620-5378-0 (sc)

Printed in the United States of America

iUniverse rev. date: 12/08/2011

TABLE OF CONTENTS

ACKNOWLEDGEMENTS

The writer wishes to express his appreciation to the following persons without whose invaluable assistance this work could not have been accomplished:

Most Reverend John J. Mitty, for permission to use the valuable Archives of the Archdiocese of San Francisco.

Sister John Mary, Archivist of the Daughters of Charity for the important material contained in their Archives at Emmitsburg, Maryland.

Reverend George A. O'Meara, Pastor of St. Raphael in San Rafael, for the use of the Baptismal Registers and the files of the Marin Journal so courteously made available by the Marin County Historical Society.

Sister M. Thomas, O.P., for the valuable material from the Archives of the Dominican Sisters of San Rafael.

Miss Sybil Power Kent and the Society of California Pioneers for their assistance.

Miss Martha Smith of the Marin County School Department for the records of 1922.

Mother M. Bernardina and Sister M. Rosalia for their valuable material in the Archives of the Dominican Sisters of Mission San Jose.

Brother Henry, F.S.C., of Mont LaSalle, Napa, for the use of the splendid Archives of the Christian Brothers.

Brother Matthew, F.S.C., of St. Mary's College, for the *Monitor* releases and references and the material on Father McKinnon.

Reverend John B. McGloin, S.J., of Loyola University, Los Angeles, and Sister M. Aurelia of Mercy High School, San Francisco for their valuable criticisms and suggestions.

Margaret Frago of St. Mary's College of Nursing, San Francisco, and John L. Gigl of St. Mary's College, California, for the many hours spent in typing the manuscripts.

Monsignor Clement McKenna of St. Vincent's for the commission to do this work and for his valuable assistance.

INTRODUCTION

The word "Orphan" means one who has lost his parents; but it also has the connotation of any neglected, forgotten, unknown child. It is in this latter sense that St. Vincent's School for Boys in San Rafael is called an "orphan".

St. Vincent's is almost unknown to San Francisco because of its location. Situated outside of San Francisco some twenty miles, that metropolis which has benefited primarily for one hundred years is almost totally unaware of its existence. Because it is outside the city limits of San Rafael by some five miles, even that city is not fully cognizant of the noble institution that has been part of its economic and community life for a century.

Because those who have administered St. Vincent's for one hundred years have chosen to carry on their work quietly, St. Vincent's has not been advertised. There have been no honorary Citizenships, no mail order solicitations. Thus this original boys town of the west has received such little notoriety that it is almost totally unknown.

It it now time on this its hundredth birthday that the story of its life be written and made known. For one hundred years it has tried to be a home for some fifteen thousand boys who have lived from one to ten years within its precincts. For one hundred years priests, brothers and Sisters have tried to be father and mother for boys whom nature or social circumstances have deprived of either their own natural father or mother or at least of a family life. For one hundred years a Christian education has been imparted to boys who would otherwise have been deprived of it. For all this time the business of raising a family of boys has gone on quietly and successfully.

In fact, so quietly has this great work been conducted that many do not actually know what boys it does care for today. Some knowing that it was originally established as an orphanage, still suppose that it is so. These forget that our modern civilization with its advances in medicine and decline in industrial accidents has very few orphaned by the death of both parents, and that modern social work would place such few children in homes rather than in an institution. In fact the number of orphans or even half orphans placed in an institution today would not warrant the maintaining of so large and elaborate an institution as St. Vincent's.

Some hearing that at one time St. Vincent's also served the Juvenile Courts of San Francisco and other counties by accepting troublesome boys, think that St. Vincent's is still some kind of correctional institution. This too is far from the truth. Because also in the past, St. Vincent's accepted boarders, children from normal homes whose parents thought they had a good reason for placing them there, many still think it is just another boarding school somewhat like its neighbors Tamalpais and San Rafael Military Academy. This too is incorrect. The St. Vincent's of the present day aims to provide a home for boys who happen to need a home. Maybe it is the death of one parent that creates the need; or it may be a temporary but prolonged illness in the family; or perhaps a divorce, the greatest home breaker of them all. But by no means does the modern St. Vincent's take delinquents. Its boys are as fine as boys anywhere. They have been unfortunate somewhere in their family life only. St. Vincent's aims to give them a temporary home and education as long as they must be away from their own family circle.

St. Vincent's is, at the end of a century, the proud boast of the Catholic Church which has maintained it since its foundation. It should be the pride of Marin County in which it is one of the show places of its marvelous environment. It is the benefactor of the thirteen Bay area counties of the Archdiocese which it has served and still serves. It is forever in the debt of the city of San Francisco for whose children it has provided a healthy home, a Christian atmosphere, and an education at great saving to the tax payers.

This work intends to tell the story, the struggles, the triumphs, the falls, the humorous and the sad events that have made up the life of this institution which has remained for one hundred years an orphan.

CHAPTER I

THE FATHER

On January 10, 1853 word went around the surrounding country side that "the Irish Giant" was dying. Don Timoteo Murphy was very sick. He lay in an upper room of his hacienda at San Rafael attended by his faithful Indian servants. Perhaps the first time one hears about this forgotten pioneer, there is wonderment at the ready mixture of Irish and Mexican and Indian terms. But all of them belonged to the one man.

First of all he was Irish. Born Timothy Murphy in the year 1800 in Coolaneck, County Wexford, Ireland, he received some business education in Dublin where he became associated with the English mercantile firm of Hartnell and Co.

Secondly he was a giant, almost six and one half feet tall, a huge man of three hundred pounds, not fat but solidly built, of great muscular strength and stamina. No wonder he was affectionately referred to as the Irish Giant.

But whence the Don Timoteo and the hacienda? Around 1826, his firm sent Timothy Murphy to Lima, Peru, where they had a branch house. After two years, Timothy Murphy came with Mr. W. Hartnell to Monterey in California to establish a beef packing plant there. Evidently this enterprise failed. But what did not fail was that Timothy Murphy won the love and admiration of everyone he met.

In 1828, California was still a Mexican possession. The Irish giant therefore became a close friend of Mexican soldiers, officers, government agents and even of the Governor Figueroa himself. When the business venture failed, Murphy turned to something more lucrative and very much in line with the sportsman he was. Living at the Presidio in San Francisco, he commenced hunting for sea otters along the Coast. It was on such a venture in company with his friend Captain Wm. Richardson who lived in Marin, that Timothy Murphy first set foot in the almost uninhabited region north of San Francisco Bay. It was Richardson who had founded the pueblo of Yerba Buena, later called San Francisco, as its first resident on June 25, 1835.

But Timothy Murphy was living in an age of great changes. Historical events were to change his life and effect his fortune. In 1833 the decree for the secularization of the California Mission system was issued by the Mexican government. One year later the actual work of spoliation, pillage and desecration began. San Rafael was one of the last affected because it was so far north, but by the time Mr. W. Hartnell made his official visit as Inspector of the Missions for the Mexican government in 1839 he found that secularization had done for San Rafael what it had done for all the other missions. The Indians in Marin were starving. Market hunters were slaughtering the game which had been the principal food for the natives; the fields which they had tilled under the direction of the Missionaries and which had provided them with grain were now bare. Few had enough clothing to cover them.

In 1839, to care for this serious situation Governor Alvarado appointed Timothy Murphy Administrator of the Mission and Agent for the Indians. Meanwhile he had become a naturalized Mexican citizen and thus assumed the name Don Timoteo. Of all the Administrators and Indian Agents in upper California, Timothy Murphy was undoubtedly the best. In order that the 1400 Indians under his care might live in peace and with some assurance of livelihood, he petitioned for a grant of land, 57,000 acres in all, arable and abounding in game and fish: "Tinicasia" he called it. It was a portion of the present Nicasio valley and Tomales Bay shoreline. The grant was given in 1841 by M. G. Vallejo. To this area, Don Timoteo as he was then universally called, moved the Indians and there, as long as he was their protector, they lived, well fed and undisturbed.

His next move was to provide for himself. In 1843 he sought for a grant of land for himself. The grant was made on February 14, 1844 by Governor Manuel Micheltorena. It was called the Rancho San Pedro, Santa Margareta and Las Gallinas, comprising almost 22,000 acres. Extending from the Rancho Nicasio on the west, eastward to the bay at San Pedro, it included much of San Rafael's present residential area to about five miles north of it. Meanwhile at the present Fourth and "C" streets he built his adobe, then the only permanent building beside the mission in San Rafael. From this hacienda he administered his affairs undisturbed for several years.

Then in 1848 came another event in history which affected Don Timoteo's life. On February 2, 1848 Mexico, by the Treaty of Guadalupe Hidalgo, was forced to cede to the United States all the territory of Texas, New Mexico, and California. Thus automatically Don Timoteo's authority as Indian Agent ceased to exist. But more than that the title of the Indians to the land granted them by Vallejo, and Don Timoteo's title to his own grant came into question. This was settled in 1852. The right of the Indians was denied; Mr. Murphy's grant was confirmed by the U. S. Land Commission. His work for the Indians came to naught, for they were dispossessed, their land sold to speculators. American vices of the gold rush era spread like wildfire among them, and in a few years, whiskey, disease, starvation, and infant mortality reduced the Indians to a few hundred.

The American occupation and the gold rush brought wealth to Don Timoteo. His lands were rich and well stocked with cattle, sheep and horses. The sale of these to the swollen population of San Francisco brought great wealth. Besides, the sportsman in Mr. Murphy, now that he had more leisure time, caused him to import a kennel of beagles, greyhounds and bird dogs. During all these years of both the Mexican and the American periods, Murphy's hacienda in San Rafael was the scene of hospitality and good humor. Although he had never married, Don Timoteo did not live alone. He had sent to Ireland for his brother Matthew a widower and two of his children, and he had his faithful Indian servants Candelerio, Jose, Alevario, and Dick. These composed the household of the Murphy hacienda.

Such was the situation on the night of January 10, 1853 when Don Timoteo was taken so violently ill. Witnesses of the events to follow testified that ill as he was, Mr. Murphy's mind was clear and sharp. He summoned his closest friends as he wished to make his will. From the village and the scattered ranches came James Black, a Scotchman and constant companion, James Miller to whom Mr. Murphy had already given a considerable grant of land, and Patrick Lambert. These three close friends were to be his executors. But there were three other men in that upper room in the hacienda that night. Al Barney the local Judge, R. K. Richards and John Davis were also present.

The first order of business was the fulfillment of an ambition of Don Timoteo's. He deeded a grant of land—about 317 acres—

across the San Rafael-Sonoma road from Mr. Miller's ranch to Archbishop Alemany, "because of the desire of Timothy Murphy to
make a donation to aid in the establishment of a Seminary or Institution of learning." The deed continued with the:

> *"express condition that the grantee shall within two years from the date
> hereof, cause a school or seminary of learning to be established and
> maintained upon said land, and cause suitable buildings to be erected
> upon said land for the use of such school or seminary of the value of
> at least one thousand dollars, otherwise this conveyance to become void
> and the land granted hereby to revert back to the grantor or his heirs.
> The grantor hereby declares that the sole object of this conveyance is
> to establish and keep up a Seminary of learning under the care and
> control of the Roman Catholic Bishop, and that when said Seminary
> shall cease to exist, this grant is to become void and the land is to revert
> back as aforesaid. Signed Timothy Murphy in the presence of A. Barney
> and R. K. Richards."*

This deed was recorded on January 13, 1853 at 8:00 A.M.

Then Don Timoteo proceeded to make his will. Judge Barney
wrote what Mr. Murphy dictated. Then he read it back to him.
The will reveals a man of deep faith, abiding principles and generous heart.

> *"In the name of God. Amen.*
>
> *I, Timothy Murphy, of San Rafael, in the county of Marin, in the State
> of California, though weak in body, yet of sound disposing mind and
> memory, in view of the uncertainty of human life, and being desirous
> of settling my worldly affairs, and directing how my Estate shall be dis-
> posed of after my decease, whenever that event may happen, do hereby
> make and publish this Instrument as my last will and testament. As a
> true believer in the Holy Catholic Faith, commending my immortal
> spirit to Him who gave it, and resigning my body to the earth, to be
> decently interned, under the directions of my executors, hereinafter
> named, I dispose of all the Estate, real, personal and mixed, of which I
> may die possessed; and all that to which I may be entitled at the time of
> my decease, in the following manner:"*

Mr. Murphy then divided his vast holdings into two parts one
of which he left to his brother Matthew and the other to his nephew
John Lucas. In his brother's portion he excepted eighty acres for
another purpose, and in John Lucas' portion he excepted the grant
made to James Miller and the grant made to "the Roman Catholic
Bishop of California for the establishment and maintenance of a

Seminary of learning". Then later in the will, Mr. Murphy provides for his Indian servants, but provides in a manner showing his knowledge of them and his wisdom in dealing with them. For although he leaves each of them a sum of money, he provides that they shall never personally receive the money, but that it be invested and the interest be used for clothing and other necessities which that money could buy for them.

This will was executed and signed at two o'clock in the morning on January 11, 1853. A few hours later the Irish Giant became unconscious and on January 13, 1853 passed to his eternal destiny.

Don Timoteo was dead. The man in whose mind and heart the future school had been conceived was dead. It was a half orphan before its birth for it had lost its father.

Chapter II

THE MOTHER

The year 1853 passed uneventfully in Marin County. The population increased only slightly. If one rode on horseback along the dusty road from San Rafael to Sonoma, only few ranches were passed. The Lucas ranch first: then the Miller's on the left; next came the Pacheco ranch and then the county line. The property for the school lay on the right across from Miller's between the road and the bay, as yet unoccupied.

When the year 1854 dawned, someone reminded the Most Reverend Archbishop Joseph Alemany of the condition in Mr. Murphy's deed. A building for the school would have to be erected this year or the land would be lost. To the Archbishop this must have seemed almost an impossibility. The site was across the bay almost twenty-five miles away. There was no means of communication. One had to go by boat, sail boat or row boat to San Rafael and then along the dusty, muddy road to the site, or else all the way by boat and up the creek which flowed through the property. How could he build a school there? There were hardly enough children to warrant it; the children of the ranch owners, yes, but then who would teach them? And what about the money needed to build the school? The Archbishop in early 1854 was himself still living in one room behind St. Francis Church. striving to build a Cathedral on the edge of town on California street. He had no money for a school so far away.

The thought occurred to him that the Sisters of Charity who had the orphanage and school on Market Street connected to St. Patrick's Church might have use for the land. These were so far the only Sisters in San Francisco, having arrived on August 18, 1852. At their head was a valiant woman, Sister Frances McEnnis, who was destined to be the mother of St. Vincent's.

Mary McEnnis, as she was named at her birth on May 19, 1812, was the daughter of Michael McEnnis and Dorothy Redmond. When she was sixteen years of age, she entered the Sisters of Charity at St. Joseph's Central House, Emmitsburg, Maryland on October 28, 1828. The next twenty-two years of her life were to be uneventful, the life of most sisters who spend their years quietly serving their Divine Master. But events were taking place in far off California which were to make her life very eventful. The gold rush brought great changes all over the United States. It was to be felt even in the quiet of St. Joseph's House in Emmitsburg, Maryland. The emigrants brought to California the dread cholera plague from the East. In October, November and December 1850, the average number of deaths per month in San Francisco was between four and five hundred. In its wake it left a host of orphan children. Priests and people were concerned what to do about them. Someone had to do something. A society was formed to raise funds and build an orphanage, but someone was needed to take care of the children. In 1852 Bishop Alemany journeyed to Baltimore, Maryland to attend the First Plenary Council there. While there he visited Emmitsburg and asked the Sisters of Charity to come to San Francisco and take charge of the orphans. The Sisters agreed to make this hazardous trip and accept the task. Seven Sisters were commissioned for this western mission and Sister Frances McEnnis was appointed Superior.

The story of their journey west is enough to prove the heroic character of this band of women. They left on June 17, 1852 traveling first to Albany where they spent ten days. On July 6, 1852 they set sail from New York for the Isthmus of Panama. The trip took ten days during which all suffered terribly from sea sickness. They still had to cross the Isthmus. For three weeks from July 16, the day they landed on the Atlantic shore, until August 5, the day they set sail into the Pacific, they all suffered indescribable hardships. They waded in mud and water and walked in torrential rains. Their clothing became soaked, their well known coronettes shapeless, they slept in so-called hotels which were filthy and without bedding. Rats ran over their beds keeping them from the rest they needed so badly. They were forced to ride men's saddles on the mules which took them over the mountains. Half the time they had to walk. Such days and nights were sufficient to break the health of the strongest women. Sister Honorine was the first to break down. The last few miles before reaching Panama City on the Pacific side, she had to be carried on a litter. The next morning at nine o'clock she died. At five that afternoon she was buried. Sister M. Ignatia was taken sick at the grave and died the next morning. She too was laid to rest in Panama.

This was quite a blow to the Superior and her now small band of four. But Panama's sufferings were to reap for them a rich harvest in their new mission. The five remaining Sisters set sail on the "Golden Gate" on August 5, and reached San Francisco on August 17.

Their sufferings were not yet ended. When they reached the shore no one seemed to expect them. On the contrary a group of men at the wharf who had never seen a Sister of Charity rudely burst out laughing at their coronettes. A carriage was obtained and the five Sisters set out for St. Patrick's Church and the orphanage. When they reached the poor building on Market Street they were to be met with another disappointment. There were no preparations for them. When Father Maginnis came out to the carriage his first words to Sister Frances were: "Are you the boss?" When they entered the two-story building they found it bare. A few wooden stools made by Father Maginnis himself and a wine barrel constituted the only furniture. Upstairs the cots were without sheets or blankets. But the kindness of Father Maginnis was to send a ray of sunshine into what seemed a foolhardy venture. He sent them the meal that had been cooked for him and the blanket from his own bed. Word of the Sisters arrival spread and help came from several sources.

The first orphan child was received on September 5, 1852. Three weeks later school was commenced with fifty girls. The rooms which served as classrooms by day were turned into dormitories at night. The boys were taught in the large room on the ground floor which was serving as a church until the separate St. Patrick's Church could be built. A regular Irish schoolmaster, Mr. Barry, taught the boys. Over this establishment presided Sister Frances.

This was the woman to whom the Archbishop turned with his problem of starting a school on Mr. Murphy's grant of land in San Rafael. The Archbishop offered to turn over the use of the property to the Sisters of Charity if they would build and maintain a school on it. He could not deed it to them but he could let them use it exclusively. In the Archbishop's own words: "I am willing at any time to write to Rome for permission to bind myself and successors to let the Sisters enjoy it forever. Deed from me to anybody might destroy the original grant altogether."

But Sister Frances could not decide this matter for herself. She wrote to her Superiors at St. Joseph's House, Emmitsburg, Maryland informing them of the Archbishop's proposition and asking what to do. She must have expected that Father Burlando, their ecclesiastical superior, and Mother Etienne Hall, their Mother Provincial, would certainly turn deaf ears after listening to the hardships they had endured so far.

To the surprise of Sister Frances and the Archbishop, word came back—"You are commanded by the Council to secure the property given to the Sisters." There was no word as to whether it was to be considered part of St. Joseph's House or an adjunct to the San Francisco foundation; that was not important now. The main thing was to secure the property, and that meant fulfilling Mr. Murphy's conditions before January 11, 1855.

Sister Frances prepared to set out at once for the new site at Las Gallinas as that portion of Don Timoteo's rancho had been called. She sought the help of Mr. John B. Redmond. He secured a rowboat manned by four Indians. In company with Mr. Redmond and Sister Corsina McKay the first trip to San Rafael was undertaken. It almost proved to be the last. So rough was the bay that Mr. Redmond himself later stated that in all his sailing days, first from Ireland to Peru, then from Peru to California, he had never experienced anything as hazardous as that trip with Sister Frances to the new site.

When they arrived Sister Frances looked over the 317 acres and selected a knoll closer to the Bay than to the road for the building. They went across the road to Miller Hall and met Mr. James Miller. He at once offered his services in helping with the erection of the building. Since the Sisters would have to live there, and since they would have to take a few boarders in order to make ends meet, the buildings would have to be more substantial and larger than the amount that Mr. Murphy had prescribed to be spent.

Mr. Miller and Mr. Kirk undertook the erection of the building. The lumber and supplies had to be hauled by ox team to the site. It was a slow and arduous task to erect the building. But through the kindness of these men, Sister Frances accomplished her task. Where she raised the $5,000 which the building cost is not known. But it is one more evidence of the genius of the woman who was destined to be the mother of the new school. Its name was obvious.

Since these good Sisters were Daughters of Charity of St. Vincent de Paul, what other name could they give the new enterprise except the name of their patron? Thus the new school would be known as St. Vincent's Seminary. It would take care of the children of the neighborhood and a few boarders to help make it financially sound. The place would be ready for occupancy by the deadline date, although both the Archbishop and the Sisters felt that an extension of the time could easily have been obtained from the heirs had they been available. But Matthew Murphy had died in March 1854, and John Lucas was in Ireland claiming the hand of Miss Maria Sweetman so that he might have a wife to share in his good fortune. Since there was no one to ask, the simplest way was to occupy before the deadline. Sister Frances McEnnis was ready. She appointed Sister Corsina McKay in charge of the new school. All was now in readiness to open.

The Building Erected by Sister Frances. Photo taken in October, 1873.

CHAPTER III

THE BIRTH

St. Vincent's was officially born on January 1, 1855 when Archbishop Alemany made the following official notation in the register of the new school:

> *"A. D. January 1, 1855*
> *The Sisters of Charity of this City, San Francisco, California, are appointed to take charge of the School of St. Vincent at Las Gallinas,. Marin County, to carry out the intention of Mr. Timothy Murphy.*
> *Joseph S. Alemany*
> *Archbishop of San Francisco"*

Sister Frances herself recorded this official opening in the following words:

> *"The Sisters of Charity from St. Joseph's House, Emmitsburg, Maryland, whose mother house is in Paris, founded a branch of their Order in Las Gallinas, on a tract of land donated to the Most Reverend Archbishop Alemany by Don Timothy Murphy. The above institution we organized under the name of St. Vincent's Seminary.*
> *Sister Frances McEnnis"*

One week later, on January 7, 1855, Sister Corsina McKay, Donna Barbara, Miss Glover and four children took possession of the property by moving into the new building. They arrived from San Francisco by boat up the creek that flowed through the property. Within a few days they opened the tiny school.

At the head of this new enterprise was Sister Corsina McKay, daughter of Bernard McKay and Catherine Byrne. She had become a Sister of Charity at Emmitsburg, Maryland on August 6, 1841. She was one of the first four Sisters to arrive in San Francisco with Sister Frances. Now she was at St. Vincent's the only religious with the two women and the children, as Sister Frances had to return to San Francisco. It was Sister Corsina's responsibility to see to it that the children were fed; the school conducted. One of her greatest hardships was the total lack of any spiritual administrations from a priest. There wasn't even Mass on Sundays as there was no priest north of San Francisco. The Mission in San Rafael was abandoned and in disrepair. In the words of Archbishop Alemany in a letter of April 15, 1855,

Sister Frances McEnnis—1812-1879—Foundress of St. Vincent's.

"There is a mission in Marin County called San Rafael some fifteen miles north of this, where there is an old miserable church, a few rooms in the same condition, and a small scattered congregation composed of Irish, American and Spanish. Within a few yards of the mission church of San Rafael is a small orchard of some two hundred yards square, now occupied by squatters."

He concludes with the modified description:

"the place is rather poor."

Thus Sister Corsina, the ladies and the children were cut off almost totally. It was a day's journey by boat to get to them, and another days trip to get back to San Francisco. Such occasional administrations as they had must have been a great source of joy. Happy indeed must have been the day when the Archbishop came for the first time. It was January 28, 1855. He visited San Rafael first and then rode out on horseback to St. Vincent's. For the first time they had Holy Mass, and for the first time Confirmation was administered to the children. The Archbishop recorded this visit as follows:

"Jan. 28, 1855
I visited San Rafael and opened the public school in Las Gallinas and confirmed in both places."

The great benefactor of Sister Corsina and the girls was their neighbor across the road, Mr. James Miller. Not only had he thrown his whole energy into building the first St. Vincent's; but now he remained the right hand of the Sisters. Truly he could be named the foster father of St. Vincent's, for without his great generosity and help the little enterprise would have surely been doomed to failure.

As it was, things were not so good. It was obvious that there were not enough children to keep a school going. Many times the few that were enrolled couldn't get there because of the winter rains and the mud which made the school inaccessible from the neighboring ranches. Meanwhile Sister Frances' superior in Maryland did not seem to approve of the idea of having boarders, for she writes in explanation to Father Borlando:

"It seems to me dear Father, I have not been understood. I do not want a Boarding school, nor have we ever had one. As the Council wished me to secure the piece of property left by Mr. Murphy, and there was no other way of doing so, but to build a house and fence the ground and

then take possession. I merely did what the will said and the law of California required. Mr. Murphy's will says there must be a school in the place, but indeed it does not say a boarding school."

Then the wise woman made a suggestion to her superiors which was to be the stroke of genius:

"Now, my Father, will you allow me to use it for the orphans, and make a branch of the orphan Asylum of it? It would be impossible to move anything to the City, as it is twenty miles from the Bay, and no road to it; we go to the place in a boat. Be assured, my father, I will not be disappointed if you don't grant it."

Evidently, Father Burlando approved of the suggestion that the place be used for the orphans, for on July 28, 1855 Sister Frances writes the following:

"Since I wrote you last, I have been over to San Rafael and took over six of the orphan girls. They have now ten orphans. I am sure, my dear Father, we feel much happier attending to our own duty than keeping a Boarding school. But really my dear Father, I thought you wanted San Rafael for an institution for St. Joseph's House, but we will be delighted to have it for our establishment. We want a quiet place sometimes. Our good Archbishop seemed delighted to have the orphans sent over. He lets us do just as we please, and if we do wrong it is our fault, not his. His wish is for us to keep our Holy Rules, and when we consult him about anything, he says, 'Keep your Rule, dear Sisters, and then you will please God, and your Bishop too'."

So an Orphanage had been born on the grounds of St. Vincent's. The ten little girls lived and went to school in the building erected by Sister Frances. But still the problem was not solved. The place was too inaccessible and the Sisters were without the services of a priest. Evidently the letters to Maryland made the Superiors feel that the project should be abandoned. In August 1855 they wrote to Sister Frances instructing her to return to San Francisco and give back the use of the property to the Archbishop. The reaction of Sister Frances is expressed in a letter she wrote on September 10, 1855:

"I have only time to say I received your two welcome letters, and feel more satisfaction in giving up Mr. Murphy's property than I have in taking it. The Sisters will be home in two days. I have spent $5000 on the property, and of course it must be lost. It is done now. I have given it up and it's no use grieving over it."

This sudden change of things put the problem of keeping a school on the property right back in the Archbishop's lap. Now what to do? It was obvious the district needed a priest. As an orphanage it seemed ideal because of the delightful climate and the healthy atmosphere. Sister Frances[1] and the Archbishop evidently reached a conclusion which gave birth to the St. Vincent's which California has known for a hundred years. They decided to send to San Rafael the boy orphans housed in the Market Street Orphanage and to put them under the care of a priest.

Meanwhile on September 12, the Sisters[2] and girl orphans gave up St. Vincent's, but left the teaching of the school under the care of Miss Maginnis, the sister of Father Maginnis, the pastor of St. Patrick's Church in San Francisco. Then the Archbishop found a priest who was willing to undertake this venture. He was an English convert, Father Robert A. R. Maurice. On September 2, 1855 a few days before the departure of the Sisters and girls, Father Maurice arrived. Within a day or two fourteen boys were sent over from San Francisco in a schooner owned by Captain Higgins. As they landed at the little wharf, Father Maurice and Mr. James Miller greeted them. The St. Vincent's Home for Boys was born.

One of the first things that occupied the attention of Father Maurice was the care of the Catholics in the county and the condition of the old mission at San Rafael. He evidently began at once proceedings for the erection of a new church, simple though it might be. Meanwhile the idea of a separate orphanage and a school for boys seems to have caught on, for at the end of 1855 the Archbishop was able to report that there were twenty-eight orphan boys under the care of Rev. Robert A. R. Maurice and a free school numbering forty pupils. We marvel at the energy of this convert English priest undertaking the financial burdens of the new orphanage[3] and trying to build a church in San Rafael at the same time with five miles of mud or dust between the two places whenever he rode into town.

On March 12, 1856 the Archbishop officially transferred Father Maurice to Stockton, a change which was not to take effect for several months. "Because Rev. Cornelius Delahunty cannot function on account of illness as Pastor of Stockton, Rev. Robert Maurice is named Pastor of the church of Stockton." When the Archbishop learned that Father Maurice had undertaken to build a new church at San Rafael, the transfer was delayed. On April 6, 1856 the Archbishop visited San Rafael and the orphanage and gave confirmation at both places. Less than a month later he returned and the event is recorded as follows:

"May 3, 1856
I visited San Rafael and blessed its new church and confirmed thirty
and visited also the orphanage of St. Vincent's for Boys.

Father Maurice[4] remained until the end of August at which time he left St. Vincent's and took up his residence in Stockton. He remains in history as the first priest director of St. Vincent's and the first pastor of San Rafael.

CHAPTER IV

EARLY YEARS

In August 1856, the Archbishop wrote in his Day book:

"The Reverend Louis Auger appointed temporary Pastor of St. Raphael and neighboring places and the charge of the orphans is given to him.."

This priest whose temporary appointment was to endure for three years has a most interesting background. He was the fourth student ordained from the little Archdiocesan Seminary of St. Thomas located at Mission Dolores, and was the first Seminarian on whom Archbishop Alemany conferred all his minor and major orders. Ordained a priest on February 16, 1856 at (Old) St. Mary's Cathedral, his first appointment was as an assistant at Our Lady of Victory Church, the French church on Bush Street; a natural appointment since he came from Paris. After a few months here he was transferred to St. Vincent's. Since the orphanage was still small the thirty-seven year old French priest devoted most of his time to the surrounding country. He was still the only priest in Marin County, and there was as yet none in Sonoma County. The people in the area around Petaluma were still without a priest. To these Father Auger turned his attention, built the first church and is listed as the first pastor. It seems a bit confusing to read the Directory for 1859—which gives the status of events in 1858.

"Male Orphan Asylum at San Rafael directed by Rev. L. A. Auger. Number of Orphans 50.
Petaluma, St. Vincent's, Rev. Louis A. Auger, Jas Lagan, Ass't.
San Rafael, St. Raphael's, attended from Petaluma."

The actual story is that both Father Auger and his assistant, Father Lagan, lived at St. Vincent's and on Saturday and Sunday took care of St. Vincent's, San Rafael and Petaluma. Considering that the road was still only a mud track, and that travel was by horseback if one took the road, and that Petaluma could be reached more comfortably only by boat, we must admire the courage and sacrifice of these pioneer priests. Father Auger gave remarkable attention to both Petaluma and San Rafael as the Baptismal books he kept for both places amply testify. Since the number of boys in his time never exceeded fifty, we doubt if he had to do any expanding at St. Vincent's. Information as to what went on from 1857 to 1859 is actually very sparse.

On May 15, 1859, Father Auger[5] conferred his last Baptism at San Rafael. The Catholic Directory for 1860—recording the events of 1859—tells us he was transferred to St. Patrick's Church, Sonora, where he was to remain until November 20, 1867 at which time he was appointed first resident Pastor of Suisun, Rio Vista, and Vacaville.

His successor at St. Vincent's was another Louis; this time a native of Belgium, Father Louis Lootens. The earliest mention of this remarkable priest is found in the Archbishop's own handwriting under date of June 29, 1857. "Reverend Louis Lootens is received into the diocese and appointed Pastor of Mariposa"; and on July 16, 1858 the Archbishop writes, "Reverend Louis Lootens appointed Pastor of Sonora and environs." His arrival at St. Vincent's was in June of 1859. His inheritance was St. Vincent's Church at Petaluma, St. Raphael's at San Rafael, and forty-six orphan boys housed and taught in the building erected by Sister Frances McEnnis. So successful was Father Lootens' administration of St. Vincent's and so thriving its condition that he is credited by many as though he were the founder and organizer of St. Vincent's. Fortunately we have personal witnesses as to the improvements made by Father Lootens. "Being artistic as well as practical, he set out many of the trees and shrubs that today (1871) add to the beauty of St. Vincent's", writes one contemporary. Aside from this, during the first four years of his administration, Father Lootens gave a great deal of attention to his vast parish, and contemporaries who have remembered him testify to the love and admiration the people of San Rafael had for him. During these first four years the terrible Civil War that threatened the very foundations of our country was being waged in the East. Although its impact on California was not too great, nevertheless its effects were felt even at St. Vincent's. The 369,000 deaths on the Federal side alone had their effect on California. Some of those men were Californians; some of their widows set out for California and died themselves leaving more orphans as their heritage. Thus around 1864 Father Lootens began to feel the pressure from the war. The population of St. Vincent's began to increase. The place was not large enough and therefore a building project was necessary.

One of the men who taught in Father Looten's school, Nicholas French, the Principal, wrote a letter on February 2, 1867 to Mr. Thomas Mooney of San Francisco in acknowledgement of a donation of one hundred dollars from the Builders Insurance Company, in which he describes these improvements of 1864:

> "During the past two years the Reverend Father Lootens, Director, has completed the additional school rooms and dormitories, capable of accommodating 140 boys. The farm which measures about 300 acres has been fenced all around, and divided by good fences into fields and gardens. The children have been supported, clothed, and educated by the Reverend Director with the limited means at his disposal, and in addition he has raised up a church in the institution capable of seating a congregation of 300 (besides the orphans) without using in its construction one cent of the orphans' fund.—The only branches of industry in which we have been able to instruct the boys are farming, gardening, etc., and the Director has heretofore considered the best course he could pursue was to push on the literary education as fast as possible to the extent which would fit the boys for learning trades, or engaging with farmers at the proper age of about fourteen or fifteen years."

We have in this letter a summary of Father Looten's activities, methods and aims.

First of all he erected the chapel and named it in honor of the "Most Holy Rosary". The cost was $3,000, money for which he gathered independently of the normal support of the institution. Secondly he built a new building costing $5,000. This is described as "a long two storied structure with a cupola in the center. The upper portion was used as sleeping apartments and the lower floor was devoted to school rooms." This was to be the Administration building in later years.

His financial circumstances were certainly strained, yet knowledge of the good work of the institution seems to have touched the hearts of many. In addition to the $100 donation of the Builders Insurance Company, there were also legacies; the earliest recorded one being a bequest of $200 from Anthony O'Connell of San Francisco on February 10, 1866, and such donations as one for $31.15 given by the Operative Boot Makers and Fitters Association of San Francisco on May 27, 1865. These were the means Father Lootens used, small though many of them were, to assist in the work. The first evidence of help from the State is recorded on March 31, 1866. "The legislature has appropriated the sum of $2,000 to the Roman Catholic Orphan Asylum located at Las Gallinas near San Rafael."

The old Administration Building erected by Father Lootens in 1864.

View of the old St. Vincent's from the main drive.

Again in March 1868 the newspaper notes an appropriation of $4,000 for the institution.

The policy of education quoted by Mr. French, the teacher, was to endure at St. Vincent's for many years. The aim was to give as much of an academic education as possible during the grammar school years and then to "farm out" the boys around the age of fourteen or fifteen. We must judge this policy not in the light of 1955 when the normal standard is not only to receive a High School education but even aspire to College, but rather in the light of 1867 when the letter was written. Actually for a boy to receive eight grades of education was the exceptional thing in 1867. Many men of later years—our fathers and grandfathers—were fortunate to get beyond the sixth grade. We see here therefore a very ambitious program on the part of Father Lootens for his boys. Being practical, the farming and the gardening not only helped the institution but also gave the boys useful knowledge and occupied their time profitably.

The year 1861 ended for Father Lootens with 133 boys in St. Vincent's. His building program, his efforts at collecting money for the institution, and his care of the parish were so great that the Archbishop came to his assistance by appointing the first regular assistant priest to St. Vincent's on January 17, 1866 in the person of Reverend Patrick Henneberry, a priest of the Congregation of the Precious Blood. During the one year of his stay, Father Henneberry assisted Father Lootens in the care of both Petaluma and San Rafael. Mass was offered every Sunday in San Rafael at 11 o'clock.

This little village at the end of 1866 is described as follows:

"December 22, 1866, San Rafael

Within the past few years, our little town has improved very much. When we first came here 15 years ago, San Rafael boasted of ten houses, besides the old mission buildings, one store, one boarding house, and one whiskey mill. The buildings were all makeshifts—not one substantial house among them except the residence of the late Timothy Murphy, now owned and used by the county as a Court House.

Now we have 3 stores, 2 hotels, 2 boarding houses, 2 livery stables, public school, an academy, a newspaper, telegraph office, 3 bootmakers, 2 blacksmith shops, butcher shop, barber, 3 lawyers and a physician. The town contains about 75 or 80 houses."

On June 10, 1866 the Archbishop visited St. Vincent's and confirmed twenty-six children and twelve in San Rafael. On this day, Father Lootens received from the Archbishop permission to take a vacation, his first since coming to St. Vincent's seven years previously. During his absence the Archbishop sent a newly ordained priest as assistant to Father Henneberry. He was the Reverend Peter Birmingham who had been ordained in December 1865.

Meanwhile Father Lootens traveled to Oregon and British Columbia spending seven months on his well-deserved vacation. While visiting at Victoria the following incident took place.

> *"Rare Painting: Reverend Father Lootens while at Victoria recently secured a valuable painting executed two centuries ago by an Italian Artist, Dominigue, representing St. John of the Cross administering the Sacrament to St. Therese. The painting was formerly the property of an English nobleman who becoming reduced in circumstances, his effects were sold and this painting became the property of a Victoria merchant who a few years ago disposed of it to a saloon keeper, from whom Fr. Lootens obtained it. It will be placed in the Chapel of the Orphan Asylum over which Fr. Lootens has charge."*

Father Lootens returned from his trip on the last Monday of January 1867. With his return there was no possibility of three priests remaining. Therefore the Archbishop moved Father Henneberry and assigned Father Birmingham as assistant at St. Vincent's. Father Birmingham seems to have taken over the Petaluma district entirely during this year 1867, and to have pushed his energies and endeavors to the coast to Tomales during 1868. Whether he continued to reside at St. Vincent's, or whether he lived at Petaluma is not certain. On July 21, 1868, the Archbishop appointed him Administrator of Tomales.

Meanwhile Father Lootens' work and zeal in San Rafael and at St. Vincent's had been so appreciated by the Holy Father in Rome that Louis Lootens had been named Bishop. A newly created Vicariate Apostolic had been erected in Idaho on March 3, 1868 and he was to be its first Bishop. News of this appointment reached San Rafael during the last week of March in 1868. The local paper carried the following item.

> *"March 28, 1868. Created a Bishop*
> *We learn that Rev. Father Lootens, the most excellent Pastor of the Catholic Church of this place has been created Bishop of Idaho. While we rejoice to hear of the advancement of the Rev. Father, we are sorry to lose him from our midst."*

On account of this sudden change in events, it was necessary for the Archbishop to appoint a new Director for St. Vincent's. He had a ready and excellent priest in Father Birmingham. He was therefore appointed on July 27, 1868 Pastor of San Rafael and Director of St. Vincent's.

The date of Bishop Lootens' departure from St. Vincent's is recorded as July 30, 1868. He was consecrated Bishop at (Old) St. Mary's Cathedral on Sunday, August 9, 1868 by Archbishop Alemany together with, as co-consecrators, Bishop Amat of Monterey and Bishop O'Connell of Grass Valley. It must have been a sad departure leaving behind the boys for whom he had been a father for almost ten years. He left to the care of his successor 146 boys, a very pretty chapel, a new building in addition to the original one and a thriving little parish in San Rafael and Petaluma. The city of San Rafael in grateful remembrance of this beloved priest named a street after him. To this day Lootens Place recalls the memory of the third pastor[6] of San Rafael.

Father Louis Lootens, Third Director—
1859-1868. Photo taken in 1868.

Father Peter Birmingham, Fourth Director—
1868-1875. Photo taken in 1874.

CHAPTER V

ADOLESCENCE

Adolescence begins normally around the age of fourteen. With the arrival of Father Birmingham as Director, St. Vincent's was well into its fourteenth year. July 27, 1868, the date of his appointment, was a fortunate day for St. Vincent's, because Father Birmingham was to prove to be an excellent Director for the growing school. Like his predecessor, Father Auger, Father Birmingham also had been ordained from the Archdiocesan Seminary at Mission Dolores. Born in Coxtown, Galway, Ireland on April 5, 1839, he emigrated to the United States with his parents when quite young. He received his education in this country and was the last one to receive his Seminary training at St. Thomas Seminary, as it closed after his ordination. He was ordained Deacon and Priest at St. Mary's Cathedral in December 1865. At about the same time as his appointment to St. Vincent's, a predecessor of his at St. Thomas Seminary, the Reverend John F. Harrington, ordained June 2, 1855 was appointed the first resident Pastor of Petaluma. Thus the care of Petaluma and Sonoma County was lifted from the shoulders of the Director of St. Vincent's.

The young energetic Peter Birmingham set to work at his new charge at once. The first item on the agenda was to remedy a situation which was to occur several times in the life of St. Vincent's. Ever since the departure of Sister Corsina McKay on September 12, 1855, the actual care of the orphan boys had been given by hired lay help. As long as the priest-Director was at home and on the job things went smoothly. But when he was away, and his parochial duties demanded him to be away often, the entire management was left to these lay people. It need hardly be pointed out that many of these over the hundred years have been most conscientious. Unfortunately even the names of many of them are lost so they cannot receive from us the credit that is their due. But also it will be readily realized that some were "time servers" and "paycheck" enthusiasts who did what they had to do only when under observation. Thus the conditions at the orphanage would not be too good. Evidently during the months of Father Lootens' vacation the lay help took advantage of his absence. The presence of Father Birmingham was not regular enough or powerful enough to keep things in good shape and besides there were now 146 boys.

Therefore the first thing Father Birmingham did was to petition the Archbishop to obtain Sisters to care for the children. This has been the wise aim of the Catholic Church through the centuries and it has always provided excellent results. The Archbishop acted at once. On August 4, 1868 he traveled to Benicia and approached the Dominican Sisters (now of San Rafael) on the subject. The record reads as follows:

"His Grace, Archbishop Alemany, held the Council of this Convent and proposed our accepting the care with Rev. P. Birmingham of the Orphan Boys at San Rafael. He, the Father of the Orphans of the Diocese, asked our aid on behalf of these little ones who were sadly neglected by the hired help in charge of them. It was agreed to send Sister Imelda Gallagher and Sister Mary Albert Hannon to the orphanage for three months when His Grace thought he might succeed in obtaining Sisters from Canada to carry on the business of the orphanage."

The first Dominican Sisters to arrive at St. Vincent's were Sister Mary Albert and Sister Mary Henry Kenney, for, on second thought, Sister Imelda, who was delicate, was not considered strong enough for the task. These two Sisters arrived on November 26, 1868. Needless to say the three months that the Dominican Sisters were to serve St. Vincent's lasted twenty-six years. By the time they would withdraw from this work, their headquarters would be at Dominican Convent, San Rafael rather than at Benicia. These Sisters took charge of the dormitories and of the boys' clothing.

The next order of business for Father Birmingham was the erection of new buildings. There were now 146 boys and even Father Lootens' building was overcrowded. Thus sometime during 1868 Father Birmingham built an addition to Father Lootens' and Sister Frances' buildings. Just how much adding the new Director did we do not know. What we do know is that he thereby went deeply into debt. To aid in reducing this indebtedness the Archbishop appealed on June 1, 1869 to the generosity of the Catholic people throughout the Archdiocese. He told in his Pastoral letter that there lay upon the Asylum a debt of some twelve to fifteen thousand, and that running expenses proportionately increased as more boys arrived.

Father Birmingham next turned his attention to his parish. The little Church at San Rafael was already too small. In October 1868, he added a gallery, "to accommodate the large and increasing congregation". But within six months it became evident that a larger and better building was necessary. On May 1, 1869, the local paper carried the following announcement:

> "ERECTION OF A NEW CATHOLIC CHURCH
>
> May 1, 1869—An effort is now being made to erect in this place a new church for the use of the Catholic Congregation of this place. The church now in use is by far too small for the requirements of the members, many of whom are unable even to obtain standing room. The new building will be erected on the lot immediately north of the graveyard, a splendid location, and is to cost from $5,000 to $7,000. Mr. O'Connor headed the list of subscribers with a gift of $1,000."

By September all was in readiness to commence work. The contract was awarded to a San Francisco contractor; the cost was to be $12,000. "The building is to be of the Gothic style of architecture and when finished will be no less an honor to our growing town than a credit to the Catholics of San Rafael." But now there was the problem of raising enough money. To assist in this matter Father Birmingham undertook to hold a Fair on October 22, 1869. This event netted some $2,446.25. The following account gives credit to those excellent people who labored for its success.

> "Receipts and expenditures of the Ladies Fair.

Miss E. J. Miller	$1,400.25
Mrs. Torres	309.75
Mrs. Barnard	216.00
Mrs. Reilly	246.00
Messrs. Ross, Boyd, Doud	245.00
Mrs. Gelligan	75.00
Mrs. Murphy	66.00
Mrs. Healey	56.00
Misses J. & F. Miller	77.00
Miss Mary J. Gordon	53.00
Miss M. A. O'Toole	50.00
Miss A. Scott	37.00
Admission to Fair	268.00
Grab Bag	183.00
Sundries	88.00
Total received	$3,357.50
Total expenses	911.25
Net	$2,446.25"

The winter of 1868-69 prevented the actual construction of the new church. Work was commenced on July 25, 1870. By October the frame building was well near completion. The following account appeared in the paper on October 8, 1870:

> *"Oct. 8, 1870—The bell for the Catholic Church now in process of erection in San Rafael, was hoisted to its place in the belfry on Wed. last. Its iron tongue being set in motion to test the ring and the tone of the metal startled some of our San Francisco sojourners who imagined they heard the sweet tones of St. Mary's Cathedral bell."*

The date for the dedication was set for October 23, 1870. At the time there was a visiting Bishop from New Zealand staying in San Francisco. He was the Most Reverend Thomas Croke, Bishop of Auckland, the brother of the Reverend James Croke, Archbishop Alemany's Vicar General. Father Croke asked the Archbishop if his brother might be permitted to dedicate the new church. Thus it was that Bishop Croke of New Zealand presided at the High Mass at 10:30, preached the sermon and gave Confirmation immediately afterwards.

Meanwhile St. Vincent's was the chief concern of Father Birmingham. The improvements he had made had been extensive and so was the debt. By April 1870, the indebtedness had reached $18,000. The people of San Francisco, whom the Institution benefited most were appealed to again. This time a Fair was proposed. It was to be held at Platt's Hall and was to last for ten days.

Aid from other sources came at this time also. For example a purse of $900 was collected in San Francisco on St. Patrick's Day at the Pavilion and the State Legislature appropriated $2,500 in April 1870. At this time the number of boys had reached 200. Their ages were from two and a half to fifteen years. Father Birmingham was kept very busy at St. Vincent's. A tribute paid to his energy in the newspapers reads as follows:

> *"Great credit is due to Fr. Birmingham for his zeal. His management of the Asylum is truly admirable. There he has wrought almost a miracle. But it must not be forgotten that his duties at the Asylum have prevented him from visiting his parishioners as frequently as he would had he no other charge than that of his parish."*

In March of 1871 the Archbishop sent as assistant to Father Birmingham a truly wonderful priest in the person of Father John Quinn (1871-1876).

There enters into the narrative at this time a note of sadness, a fact which is part of life but which due to the progress of medicine is rare in our times. It was the death of one of the boys. Whether he was the first one to die, we do not know. The Marin *Journal* records it on January 21, 1871 in the following words: "One of the inmates of the Orphan Asylum, a little boy named 'Mack' died at that institution on Saturday last." This terse notice tells the story. Another such notice on May 22, 1873 is even more impersonal. "A lad of four years died at the Roman Catholic Orphan Asylum San Rafael on the 16th, whose name we have not learned." Perhaps these children died nameless to the general public, but the pain felt by their loss to Father Birmingham and to Father Quinn, and the Sisters must have been very deep. Certainly it was not their fault. Evidence down through the years pays eloquent tribute to the health of the children in general. But these occasional deaths did occur. Their happening gave rise to the little cemetery, still on the grounds, where lie the remains of four Christian Brothers and several children, all nameless.

CHAPTER VI

GOING TO SCHOOL

We are fortunate at this time to have a personal eye witness description of St. Vincent's. The Editor of the San Rafael *Weekly Herald* sent a reporter to visit St. Vincent's on October 29, 1874. Although neither Father Birmingham nor Father Quinn were at home on this occasion, the principal of the school, Mr. Mullany escorted the reporter through the institution. Following is the account:

"We visited first the school rooms, four in number capable of accommodating more than 300 pupils. It being noon day, the rooms were empty; we passed directly thru the suite and out at a back door into the playyard where 280 youngsters were gathered ages 4 to 14. The yard is surrounded by a plank fence with a roof resting on it, which enables the boys to pass entirely around in wet weather without being exposed. Under the school rooms is the wash room where 100 tin basins stand ready for use in a long line of sinks which surround the room. 280 towels, each with a number on it, hang ready for use by their respective owners. On the other side we found a commodious bathroom which has a capacity for bathing with hot or cold water all the boys once a week. From the bathroom we passed upstairs to the refectory.

7 barrels of flour a week are baked into very wholesome bread, and 2 bullocks furnish meat during the same time; to which is added a most bountiful supply of vegetables raised on the place, and the milk of 40 cows. The cook stood by a French range and the baker exhibited his huge oven.

2 great windmills whirl their arms when there is sufficient breeze and exert their force in pumping water to the tanks on the hill; when the wind fails a horse power is ready for use which is also utilized in the laundry adjoining, in revolving the washing machine. From the laundry we go back to the main buildings again and up the stairs to the dormitories. The snowy little beds, arranged in long and regular lines, were models of cleanliness. In or adjoining each dormitory, (there are several) one or more grown persons sleep to insure order. Downstairs the very smallest are kept. From the infants room we go to the room where the clothes are kept. A large number of big pidgeon holes are arranged around the room, each having a number on it, to which a boy answers. The owner of each depository here stores his spare jacket, hat and boots. We were painfully impressed with the meagre wardrobe of these little men. An old straw hat, not worth a dime was carefully stored inside on an ancient pair of trousers."

Perhaps the poverty of clothing can be easily recognized when we recall that Father Birmingham seems to have been constantly harrassed by a shortage of funds. The struggle to make ends meet was particularly difficult during the years 1870-1875. His only sources of support were the allotments from the State and donations by individuals.

A report in the *Marin County Journal* of March 2, 1876 shows the support given by the State during the years 1871 to 1875 inclusive. The State allowed the magnificent sum of $75 a year for whole orphans and $50 a year for half orphans and for abandoned children. This support was given in allotments of $18.75 and $12.50 per child per quarter. Thus the huge ledger books still at St. Vincent's today show the entire student body as listed every three months when filing for State support. The State also generously granted "aid" for specific purposes several times during these years. Each grant of aid required a special appropriation from the State Legislature. The amounts granted by the State for "support" and as "aid" are recorded in the article of March 2, 1876. The paper stated that the anual expenses at St. Vincent's were about $40,000. It then listed the State's support commenting on the fact that St. Vincent's received more than any other asylum because it was the largest in the State.

```
"1871—March 22nd—Support of inmates................... 4,657.71
    May 17th—Support of inmates................... 1,645.41
    June 30th—Aid ................... 312.50
    June 30th—Aid ................... 625.00
    October 11th—Aid ................... 312.50
    October 11th—Support of inmates ................... 1,635.14
    November 8th—Aid ................... 1,791.14

1872—January 15th—Aid ................... 312.50
    January 20th—Support of inmates ................... 1,811.72
    April 9th—Aid ................... 312.50
    May 14th—Support of inmates ................... 1,840.80
    June 29th—Aid ................... 312.50
    October 11th—Aid ................... 750.50
    November 6th—Support of inmates ................... 1,806.80
    November 6th—Support of inmates ................... 1,920.00

1873—January 9th—Aid ................... 750.50
    February 5th—Support of inmates ................... 1,992.44
    April 9th—Support of inmates ................... 1,811.89
    April 9th—Aid ................... 750.00
    June 7th—Aid ................... 750.00
```

July 12th—Support of inmates	1,734.00
October 8th—Aid	750.00
October 8th—Support of inmates	1,699.03
1874—January 8th—Aid	750.00
January 10th—Support of inmates	1,641.80
April 8th—Aid	1,500.00
July 7th—Support of inmates	1,730.42
August 18th—Support of inmates	1,838.23
November 25th—Support of inmates	3,322.95
1875—February 2nd—Support of inmates	3,267.62
April 20th—Support of inmates	3,202.61
July 20th—Support of inmates	3,382.76
October 21st—Support of inmates	3,382.76

This was a total of $53,905.19 for five years. Yet, if as the same article states, the expenses were $40,000 per year, we have the grand total of expenses for these years reaching the huge sum of $200,000. State assistance therefore met only one fourth of the cost during those years.

The rest had to be met by private means. We note therefore, in those same years, a Fair in 1873 in San Francisco at Platt's Hall which was regarded as very successful. We read of annual collections throughout the Archdiocese called for by the Archbishop. We also find record of generous Christmas gifts, the most outstanding being that of Mr. C. D. O'Sullivan who gave $500 each Christmas for several years. The most generous single donation was received at Christmas in 1875 from Alvinza Hayward for $2,500 together with a $500 donation from James C. Flood. Another circumstance that favored Father Birmingham is told in the following notice:

> *"The Board of Equalization was in session three days last week. They reduced the assessment of the Roman Catholic Orphan Asylum from a little over $9,000 to $5,000."*

Thus the Director had $1,000 less taxes to worry about from then on. In spite of these means of assistance, St. Vincent's was $35,000 in debt by the end of 1874.

To complete the story of Father Birmingham's efforts on behalf of St. Vincent's, we must turn our attention to the school program as it evolved under his care. Evidently God's favor was upon him, for he secured in 1872 the services of a gentleman who was to be the

Principal and one of the teachers for many years, and who won for himself the admiration of all. He was Mr. John Mullany. The local weekly paper speaks of him on August 12, 1872 in the following manner:

> "Mr. Mullaney, the Principal of the school, is a teacher of extraordinary ability and success. The proficiency of his pupils is marvelous A gentleman told us that he had attended the examinations of many schools for the past fifteen years, but never had he seen such scholarship as was displayed by Mr. Mullaney's boys. Lads of 13 and 14 worked the most difficult and intricate problems. The examination in arithmetic extended through all business arithmetic, U.S. stocks, profit and loss, interest, duties, general average, discount, foreign and domestic exchange, equation of payment, partnerships: and had not time failed, these little fellows would have ciphered through Robinson's University edition to binomial theorem. Not parrot-like either. Their analysis of the problems evinced a thorough mastery. Questions by visitors did not confuse them. They understood their work. We would not disparage Mr. Mullaney's position but it seems to us that he is hiding his light under a bushel. He should be at some grand educational institution where his field would be commensurate with his genius. He is also a law student, and studied three years with the Hon. T. J. Hendricks of Indiana."

This is as much as we know about Mr. Mullany, except that he continued to let his light shine at St. Vincent's until 1876 and then later returned until 1878. It was under his care that the Annual examination commenced and became the big day of the year in the life of St. Vincent's. On the day of the Annual Examination crowds of people came to St. Vincent's from San Francisco. On July 30, 1873, the day of the Annual Examination, the steamer *Contra Costa* had to make an extra round trip from San Quentin because of the crowds that came to St. Vincent's for the affair. The day was marked by an ambitious program and then the visitors were the guests of St. Vincent's for the noon meal. In 1874, this program took place on July 30, but in 1875 it was postponed one week until August 5 on account of the twenty-fifth anniversary of the Archbishop. In 1876 it was not held until August 18, and in 1877 it was omitted on account of the building program. Year after year it continued to be the finest day in the year, and its celebration lasted almost annually until about 1920. A detailed description tells us what this day was like. The list of dignitaries present on July 30, 1874 included the following:

Reverend Archbishop Alemany, Rev. Fathers Gibney, Powers, Slattery, Morrissey, Keiley and Nattini, S.J., of San Francisco, Kelly of Folsom, Callaghan of Sacramento, Carroher of San Rafael, Cleary of Petaluma, Brother Justin of St. Mary's College, Brother Patrick, Assistant General of the Order of Christian Brothers of Paris; Messrs. C. D. O'Sullivan, F. D. Eagan, Gustave Touchard, Hon. P. A. Roach, Doctors Gibbon and Sharkey, P. J. Sullivan, John Brougham, James Phelan, wife and family; Mrs. Mullen, F. S. Weninger and wife, James Daley, wife and daughter; Miss Clara Hopkins, John Barry and wife, and Mrs. and Dr. William Jones, all of San Francisco; Senator Duffy of Sacramento; Mrs. General Schofield, Mrs. M. J. O'Connor, Miss Annie Rosecrans; John Lucas and family, T. Day and family, James Miller, wife and daughters; J. B. Redmond, wife and daughters; A. Lawson, P. Owen and family, E. B. Mahon, J. Wolfe, J. J. Schneider, J. O'Connor and ladies, M. Murray, E. Mandel and wife, H. B. Bass, James Sheppard, Miss Ella Sheppard, W. M. Boyd and family, and others from this county.

The exercises were held in one of the large classrooms. The guests occupied the students desks. The 280 boys sat in front on improvised seats which were banked almost to the ceiling. The program commenced with a selection by the fourteen piece school Band playing "Hail to the Chief". Next followed a song by the assembled boys, and then an address called the Salutatory by Charles Trainor who was described as "self-possessed and manly without any appearance of vain glory and whose rendering of the text was intelligent and forcible". The Band then played another piece after which Dan Lawler read an essay on "The German Question". The atmosphere of scholarship after such a profound thesis was cleared by James Desmond who sang as a solo, "The Harp That Once Thru Tara's Halls".

Then the program got down to business. The examination in Ancient History took place. At its conclusion the Band rendered "Marching Thru Georgia". John Keon followed with the reading of an essay. John was remarked on by the visitors because he walked with the aid of a crutch having lost the use of one leg. The clarity and brightness of the boy's intellect seemed all the more acute because of his misfortune. James Desmond now returned to the stage with a companion, T. Lloyd, where both sang a duet.

The examination in Arithmetic followed; it was in turn followed by the Band rendering "The Red, White, and Blue". Frank Wilson next read an essay on "The Church". Daniel Lawlor sang

"Hail Columbia" and the examination in Algebra took place. The entire student body then sang a song for the close of school. But it was not yet the close. The program continued with the Examination in Physical Geography and was in turn followed by another memorized speech by Stephen Killiha. A final school song was followed by a Valedictory spoken by John Ledwidge. This speech was printed in full in the newspaper; obviously written by Mr. Mullany it manifests deep erudition and scholarship as it pays tribute to Catholic education, to the Archbishop for maintaining such a school as St. Vincent's, to Father Birmingham and a farewell to his schoolmates.

The Archbishop then addressed the crowd; and after his remarks called upon the Honorable Philip A. Roach. This gentleman had evidently been closely associated with St. Vincent's since Bishop Lootens' time. He himself, in his talk described how in those days as first President of the St. Vincent's Orphan Asylum Society he had often crossed the bay when it was rough and boisterous in a small sailboat to look after the interests of St. Vincent's. Mr. Roach also, together with Senator Duffy had pioneered the campaign for state aid. Father Birmingham, noting the length of the program with its twenty items and the talks of the dignitaries stood up then and said simply: "Friends. Now that our exercises are over, we invite you one and all to go with us to the dining room and partake of dinner. And if anyone fails to accept our invitation, we will feel hurt. Please, come, all!"

One year later, the program was quite similar with eight Band numbers, the Examinations in Geography, U. S. History, Arithmetic, Algebra and Grammar. The opening welcome was given by William Kelly, the speeches by George Callan, John Costello, Charles Trainor and Dan Lawlor, the Valedictory by P. O'Neil and the soloists were Dan Lawlor, Charles Trainor and James Desmond.

The cultivation of music has always, even to the present day, been an important part of the training of the boys at St. Vincent's. The Band and the Choir have been well known throughout the Bay Area over the century of its life. The first evidence of a Band was the fourteen piece affair of 1874. Evidently Father Birmingham recognized the fact that every child must be able to excel in some field in order to achieve a true emotional balance. Some children do very well in school subjects; others excel in athletic events; others receive the satisfaction that their hearts crave because they can draw or make things. But music is for many the only satisfaction because they have an inherent sense of rhythm. Thus the band at St. Vincent's has helped hundreds of boys achieve emotional stability for almost one hundred years.

It seems as if Father Birmingham in his excellent administration of the internal affairs of St. Vincent's had wisdom and foresight unequaled by his many successors. But Father Birmingham's days at St. Vincent's were coming to a close.

CHAPTER VII

FAST GROWTH

On March 4, 1875 the following article appeared in the San Rafael weekly, the *Marin Journal.*

> *"Wanted: A Resident Priest.*
>
> *The labors of the President of St. Vincent's Orphan Asylum are arduous, and demand the constant attention of an able man. The Catholic parish of San Rafael is wealthy and populous, extends over a wide area and would seem to require the services of a learned and devoted member of the holy priesthood. These two positions are devolved upon one man. Rev. Father Croke has been appointed to the post, and Rev. Father Birmingham will remain a few weeks to assist the new incumbent in his untried duties. Father Birmingham has not yet been assigned to any post. He is universally esteemed and beloved in this community where he has toiled so long, and we would take the liberty to suggest that his appointment as resident priest of the parish of San Rafael would fill the members of the Church with grateful feelings to the Archbishop, and do very much to advance the interest of the parish. Few men are so fortunate in winning golden opinions from all classes as he has been, and the thought of his departure seems almost intolerable. This arrangement would also be to the advantage of the Asylum in giving Father Croke more leisure to attend to its interests."*

This was quite an encomium. especially from a weekly paper which almost totally ignored the Catholic Church. This article more than anything else shows the love and esteem in which Father Birmingham was held by the people and the children. Needless to say the Archbishop was not influenced to leave Father Birmingham as Pastor of San Rafael. Another article, published the same day describes St. Vincent's as it was at the departure of Father Birmingham:

> *"One of the most attractive spots in the environs of San Rafael is that on which stands the home of the orphan boys, known as St. Vincent's, on the Petaluma road. The healthfulness of the spot is equal to its beauty, which is attested to by the entire absence of sickness, though there are at present 260 boys. Father Birmingham has been in the position of President for seven years, during which time the institution has had uninterrupted prosperity, and has done a noble work both for the state, and for the homeless and friendless little fellows who have enjoyed its privileges. Father Birmingham has made his influence felt, no less by his tender and loving personal care for the boys, than by his*

*wise administration of the business affairs of the Asylum, and his relin-
quishing the place is a matter of deep regret to all."*

The excellence of the school under the direction of Mr. Mullany, the "scrupulous neatness of the place in all its appointments" under the care of the Dominican Sisters, the "universally
cheerful and happy faces of the boys" all these things attest to the
thriving and wholesome condition of St. Vincent's as Father Birmingham turned it over to his successor.

This change, so lamented by all, actually occurred on February 22, 1875, the date on which the Archbishop appointed Father
James Croke, Pastor of San Rafael and Father Birmingham, Pastor
of St. Joseph's Church in San Francisco. Father Birmingham's appointment did not become public knowledge until April as he
remained over to assist Father Croke in getting established. At the
moment of the appointment there were several items of unfinished
business. For example, an addition of twenty-seven feet was being
added to the Chapel in order to increase its capacity. Besides the
whole building was being raised four feet. Mr. John Sims was the
contractor. Plans were also being made for the construction of
another building to house the increasing number of boys. Finally,
by April 2, 1875, Father Birmingham was ready to leave. His many
admirers in San Rafael surprised him and gave him a purse of
$540 as an expression of their esteem. Thus ended the regime of
Father Peter Birmingham.[7]

At the time of his succession, Father James Croke was fifty
years of age and a veteran of twenty-six years in the priesthood. Tall
and erect of stature, well built and graceful in bearing, he brought
to his office a treasure of experiences and the wisdom that comes
from that school.

He had been born in Kanturk, County Cork, Ireland in 1825
of a Catholic father and a Protestant mother. He received his early
education in the local school of Charleville, County Cork. For his
priestly studies he was sent to the Irish College at Paris. By 1847,
James Croke was ready to be ordained; but since he was too young
the ordination had to be postponed. In the same year Bishop Francis
Norbet Blanchet of Oregon visited the Seminary looking for priests
for the northwest. James Croke volunteered. He was finally ordained in 1849 and on this occasion his mother was received into
the Church. The deep piety of his family was reflected in the fact

that his brother was also a priest, and eventually a Bishop, and his sister was a Sister of Mercy in Australia.

Father James Croke left for Oregon after his ordination and arrived in San Francisco in 1850, at a very crucial moment. The tiny gold rush camp was at the moment in the midst of a cholera epidemic. Father Croke found one priest in San Francisco, the Rev. Anthony Langlois ministering to the needs of the dying. With the generosity that was always his, he joined his fellow priest in the dangerous work of caring for the cholera patients. In 1851 he left for Oregon. The city of Portland hails him as the first priest to build a church in what is now a thriving metropolis. Father Croke found no thriving metropolis, but rather a scattered and heavily wooded area. He himself helped not only in felling the timber but in the actual construction of the new church which he named Immaculate Conception. He lived in the rear in an 8 by 12 room.

Father James Croke, Fifth Director of St. Vincent's—1875-1888.

From such headquarters he went out into the surrounding country of southern Oregon on his missionary journeys. In a letter to his brother the Bishop many years later he described one such missionary journey, one which took him East to the Missouri river.

> "In company with a Jesuit missionary I traveled in 1855 from Portland through the Cascade and Rocky mountains clear on to the Missouri river. When I returned to Portland in the spring of 1856, I had traveled on horseback 3,600 miles. From the time I left the last white settlement in Oregon, one hundred miles east of Portland, until I reached Fort Benton on the Missouri river, a distance of 1,800 miles, we met only nine white men, six Jesuits, two Canadian trappers and a half breed scout."

Such missionary journeys proved too much for the health of Father Croke. On returning from the trip above, he was in serious condition. It was decided that he should return to California. On his arrival he was appointed by Archbishop Alemany to St. Mary's Church in Oakland of which he became the first Pastor. After two years he was transferred to the Cathedral in San Francisco (Old) St. Mary's, where he served as Pastor and Vicar General for eleven years. Finally in 1875 his health became so poor that he asked to resign the office of Vicar General. Because of the excellence of the climate and because of his ability, the Archbishop appointed Father Croke to the task of enlarging and improving St. Vincent's.

Father Croke has been described as being a man generous to a fault, gentle and kind and beloved by all. We shall see these qualities unfold as we proceed with the story of St. Vincent's under his guiding hand. The task that lay before him was no small one. St. Vincent's lay under a debt of $35,000, as already mentioned. Besides, the number of children requiring care was rapidly increasing, thus necessitating an enlargement of the place. There were at this time 280 boys.

One of the hardships that faced Father Croke was the loss of the beloved Father John Quinn, assistant to his predecessor and to Father Croke. It was in January 1876 that Father Quinn's health failed and he had to leave for the hospital in San Francisco. Father Cassin was sent to assist during the illness of Father Quinn. After two months it became obvious that Father Quinn was not going to get well. Finally on March 1, 1876 death took this beloved priest.

In his will he left all his books to John Mullany, the Principal of the school. He left $250 to St. Vincent's and a like sum to Sister Frances McEnnis for the girls' orphanage in San Francisco. His two colts he gave to the Murray brothers, John and Michael Jr. The loss of Father Quinn in March 1876 was to be followed by the loss of Mr. Mullany who resigned. Yet in spite of these set backs and disappointments, Father Croke proceeded with plans to expand St. Vincent's. The following notice appeared in the paper on April 13, 1876:

> *"April 13, 1876, St. Vincent's Orphanage. This institution with accommodation for only 250 boys is at present caring for 280 and is of course in a very crowded condition. It is in the plans and hopes of the managers of this great charity to erect new buildings of brick for the use of the home and school, and utilize the present structures as workshops. On the occasion of Archbishop Alemany's silver jubilee a few months since, he was presented with a magnificent span of horses and carriage. Father Croke tells us that as soon as he can complete the arrangements this splendid turnout is to be raffled for the benefit of the St. Vincent's Orphanage. Notice will be given, so that all can have an opportunity to secure tickets, which will be put at a very low figure."*

Whether this raffle materialized or not, there is no evidence. But we do know that the plans for expansion did materialize. In August, 1876 the construction began on an addition, not of brick as hoped for, but of wood, a two story addition, "to the main building on the West 100 by 30 feet, the upper floor to be used as a dormitory and the lower floor for additional school rooms and offices". An addition was also made to the dining room. As previously the contract was awarded to Mr. John Sims. The cost price was estimated at $10,000. Construction went on during September and October and into the winter months. At last in January they were nearing completion. Finally the date of dedication was set for February 22, 1877. The newspaper told the story as follows:

> *"February 22, 1877. Dedication at the Asylum.*
>
> *The additions and improvements at St. Vincent's Roman Catholic Orphan Asylum for Boys are now completed and the dedication ceremonies will be held at noon today (Thursday). Archbishop Alemany, Bishop Moreno, of lower California and other dignitaries of the church will be present and assist.*
>
> *The Asylum now has accommodations for 400 boys. One dormitory alone has 202 beds. An addition has been built 100 feet long, two stories high, affording a new school room, and a thirty foot addition has been*

View of the old St. Vincent's from the rear, as seen from the railroad, showing long south wing erected by Father Croke in 1878.

The old St. Vincent's from the rear, showing part of the north wing.

made to the main building. The improvements, with the additional furniture, have cost about $14,000, all of which Father Croke has paid. Mr. Sims' contract alone for carpenter work was $8,000.

Mr. Mullany, the former teacher, has consented to resume his place as Principal of the school, and will take charge very soon. We believe that Mr. Mullany has no superior as an instructor, or a disciplinarian, and we heartily congratulate the institution on his return."

The story for the next few years is a repetition of the above— more boys — more new buildings — more money expended, but somewhere and somehow inevitably obtained by Father Croke. The addition built at the end of 1876 was followed by another of similar size at the end of 1877. This one, described as 100 by 25 feet, was to be "furnished with boxes to keep the boys' clothes". The total number of boys in September, 1877 was 370. More and more demands were made on Father Croke, and no one was refused. This too rapid expansion and too many boys was to be his undoing, but the generous heart never said no. After all, there was no other place to take care of these boys; therefore Father Croke felt that he had to take them. During the quarter from January 1 to April 1, 1878 he took in forty boys. The number was now 400. Now the Chapel was too small, the water supply too inadequate; everything had to be expanded and enlarged. In the spring of 1878 he turned his attention to the water problem. A new tank 12 feet high and 15 feet in diameter, capable of holding 12,500 gallons was built. Meanwhile he was planning a reservoir, with water to be piped from the hills behind the Miller ranch. A pipe one and a quarter miles long, costing $4,000 would supply the reservoir.

In August, 1878, Father Croke began the construction of a third wing one hundred feet in length. The following spring he made arrangements with the Archbishop that all these new and extended buildings should be blessed. The date was set for July 23, 1879. The local paper describes the dedication as follows:

"Last Wednesday the early boat brought a large delegation of guests and friends of the Institution, the Petaluma train conveyed the majority of them to the Asylum, and at 9:30 the ceremony of blessing the recently constructed and commodious buildings commenced. Rev. Father Croke attended by two Acolytes lead the Procession, the Archbishop and 35 Priests and Brothers succeeding, chanting the blessing, the congregation following. After the Chapel had been formally dedicated according to the impressive rites usual to the Catholic church, Mass was cele-

brated by Rev. P. Callaghan, O.P., which was immediately followed by the Archbishop's deep, logical sermon, after which the Sacrament of Confirmation was given to 98 boys.

At 1 P.M. the orphan's lunch satisfied the appetites of 405 little fellows who look the picture of health. During their repast, we strolled through the different apartments and were inexpressibly pleased with the well managed, well ventilated and cleanly kept dormitories, one of which measures 215 feet long and contains 210 beds. Another dormitory extends from this across to the opposite wing and is 80 x 24 feet, while the wing is 245 x 30 feet.

At 2 P.M. a cordial invitation by Father Croke called all visitors to a bounteous banquet. At 5 P.M. the down train carried away the departing guests."

Within one year the paper announced that Father Croke was hard at work with further improvements and contemplated building. On June 10, 1880 the following article appeared:

"Father Croke is making extensive improvements at the Orphan Asylum. A large force is employed in grading and widening the avenue which leads to the Asylum, and in cutting down the knoll on which the Chapel stands. A part of the Chapel will be removed and utilized for literary purposes, and a new chapel, much larger, will take its place."

One year later, on June 23, 1881 the paper carried the following announcement:

"The Most Rev. Archbishop Alemany will dedicate the new Church at the Boys Orphanage near San Rafael on Wednesday, June 29th at 10 A.M., and will administer Confirmation on the same day. The cars leave San Rafael at 8:25 and leave the Asylum returning at 5 P.M."

The Chapel of the Holy Rosary—
dedicated June 29, 1881.

Interior of the Chapel.

This Chapel on the hill with its tall spire was to be a landmark for many years. It would be the last of the buildings to be replaced. The dedication was recorded in the Monitor of July 7, 1881:

"CHURCH DEDICATION AT THE ORPHAN ASYLUM

On Thursday, the Feast of Sts. Peter and Paul, a new Church lately erected at the San Rafael Orphan Asylum, was solemnly dedicated to divine worship by Archbishop Alemany assisted by Bishop Raimundi of Hong Kong, who is stopping for a short time in California on his way to Europe. The school year of the institution was closed on the same day, and both events attracted a large number of visitors from San Francisco as well as from the country around. The dedication procession began at 10 o'clock and was followed by Mass at which the chanting was executed by the choir of the boys with a skill remarkable indeed, especially for such youthful musicians. After Mass the Sacrament of Confirmation was administered to about 160 boys by the Bishop of Hong Kong. About the same number had previously made their first Communion in the morning. Preparatory to the administration of the sacraments a Retreat had been given during the week to the orphans by the Dominican Fathers from Benicia, four of whom remained at the Asylum for that purpose.

The new church is cruciform, the longer arm of the cross being forty feet wide and sixty eight long, and the arms extending some twenty feet on each side. The sanctuary is shallow but the same width, and a covered passage runs behind it. The interior is finished in plain white plaster with a groined roof, but the sanctuary is ornamented by a handsome stained glass window, the work of John Mallon of this city, and the altar is richly gilt and painted and forms a fine contrast to the simplicity of the other parts of the church. The dimensions will afford accommodations to at least twice the number of boys now in the Asylum, and ample provision of doors is made for their speedy entrance or egress.

The front is ornamented by a tower and a spire, the latter surmounted by a richly gilt cross, which is conspicuous for miles owing to its elevated position."

This was the crowning achievement of Father Croke's years of building and expansion at St. Vincent's. For fifty years it was the center of all the religious life of the institution. It, best of all, symbolized his life of dedication to the works of mercy which went on within the walls of St. Vincent's.

CHAPTER VIII

A DECADE OF ACTIVITY
1877 - 1887

After reading the record of expansion in buildings the obvious question concerning the source of finances comes to mind. The answer is, of course, not fully known; but its accomplishment was part of the genius of Father Croke. We do have some record of gifts which certainly helped. One of them was of such generosity that it probably paid for several of the buildings. It was a legacy of $50,000 from William O'Brien of Bonanza fame in May, 1878. No wonder we read that a Solemn Pontifical Requiem Mass was offered in St. Vincent's Chapel on June 7, 1880 for the soul of the late William S. O'Brien. Another legacy of $5,000 was left in February, 1879 by Mr. Clark of San Francisco. No other large donation is recorded until Christmas of 1884 when Senator Fair gave a gift of $2,500 for the occasion. It was such generosity on the part of individuals, including many whose names are unknown, that aided Father Croke in the tremendous expansion of the years 1876-1881.

Father Croke had other work for which he needed aid. For one thing, he was Pastor of an enormous parish which included San Rafael, Nicacio, Bolinas and Sausalito. To aid him in this work the Archbishop always kept an assistant priest at St. Vincent's. Father Cassin was the last one we referred to. After a stay of two years he was transferred in July, 1877 to St. Patrick's in San Francisco. A Father Nealand of New Zealand stayed to assist for the summer. He was replaced by Father William Power for the month of September, then on October 5, 1877, the Archbishop appointed Father Cassin's successor in the person of Father John Kemmy. This priest remained as assistant to Father Croke until November 20, 1878 when he was transferred to St. Brigid's.

It was during the days of Father Kemmy that a great change took place affecting transportation between St. Vincent's and San Francisco. Since 1876, construction had been underway on a railroad connection between Petaluma and San Rafael. Previous to that time, Petaluma residents reached San Francisco by taking a train to Donohue, a wharf some eight or ten miles below Petaluma on the River and thence by boat to San Francisco; San Rafael residents took a short train ride to San Quentin and thence by boat to San Francisco. Residents of the area in between San Rafael and Petaluma were without direct transportation. This was solved by the completion in 1878 of a connecting line between Petaluma and San Rafael. This railroad ran right through St. Vincent's property and stopped at a station common to St. Vincent's and to Mr. Miller and called "Miller Station". The railroad was a great attraction for the boys. But it became a positive thrill when the owner, Colonel Peter Donohue sent down to St. Vincent's on September 11, 1878 a brand new engine and nine new passenger cars to take the boys on an excursion to the Redwoods in Sonoma county. One can imagine the thrill and joy of that trip for the boys. St. Vincent's benefited also from the railroad in still another way. Excursions and picnics became the usual thing for organizations. One such excursion picnic in September, 1878 from Sonoma, sent all the left-overs by special car to Father Croke for his boys. The donation included two hundred pounds of meat, two hundred large loaves of bread, two hundred dozens eggs and numerous boxes of cakes and other delicacies. Of course the greatest benefit derived from the railroad was transportation. Visitors could now take the boat to Pt. San Quentin and then the train to St. Vincent's. What took Sister Frances McEnnis a full day in a row boat, less than twenty-five years ago, now took about two hours.

Shortly after the inauguration of the railroad, Father Kemmy was moved and succeeded by Father M. O. Riordan. It was during his days with Father Croke that a new problem arose pertaining to the church in San Rafael. The town passed an ordinance in 1879, that there were to be no more burials in the cemeteries in town. This meant that a new cemetery had to be acquired. Father Croke succeeded in acquiring a site about half way between town and St. Vincent's. In May, 1880, trees were being planted in the new cemetery in order to beautify it.

At this same time, Father Croke had a burial in his new cemetery which brought great sorrow to St. Vincent's because it affected a much loved family, the Millers. Miss Julie Miller, one of Mr. Miller's daughters, died on May 30, 1880. Her funeral was held from St. Vincent's old chapel on Thursday morning, May 6, 1880.

This untimely loss caused grave illness to her mother whose decline set in a few weeks after Miss Julie's loss. Such sorrow to the heart of James Miller, the kindly foster-father of St. Vincent's was reflected at St. Vincent's.

Another project, either of Father Croke or of one of his assistants, was the establishment of a Catholic school in San Rafael. It was a school modeled after the Catholic schools in Ireland. Not staffed by Sisters, this one room school had a Catholic teacher in 1880, named Mrs. Harcourt. It was held in the old Church built by Father Maurice. How long it succeeded in lasting we do not know. Again in December, 1883, we read of the opening of the second session on January 2, 1884, "under the able and successful teacher, Mr. J. C. Robinson." Such schools were common in the early days in California but their existence depended totally on the ability of the priests to find such a teacher. As they came and went, the school opened and closed.

Meanwhile further progress was made in the parish by the building and dedication of a tiny church in Sausalito in January, 1881. This year, 1881 saw Father M. O. Riordan moved and Father Edward Slevin sent to assist Father Croke until January, 1882. At that time Father P. Scanlan came for a period of eight months.

The year 1882 was marked by only two things. The arrival of Father P. R. Lynch as assistant in August, 1882, and the sad death of Mrs. Miller on December 26, 1882. Her funeral, like her daughter's was held from St. Vincent's, but this one from the new Chapel on the hill.

The energy of Father Croke was still not used up in spite of the building program which had terminated in the new Chapel in 1881. Again in 1882, he was making plans. On May 25, 1882 the following article appeared in the local paper:

> "Rev. Fr. Croke will reclaim about 400 acres of tideland near the Asylum this year by the same method employed at Novato Meadows, that is, with an immense ditching machine. About 40 acres reclaimed last year is in potatoes which are looking well. Hereafter all new land will be sown in alfalfa."

The year 1883 brought with it several items of major importance. The first was the visit on May 28, 1883 of the Archbishop on which occasion he gave the Sacrament of Confirmation to 210 boys. This was by far the largest confirmation class in the history of the institution. The second event was of a serious nature, an epidemic of typhoid fever. The newspaper records it as follows:

> *"August 2, 1883. Quite a number of cases of Typhoid occurred recently at St. Vincent's Orphan Asylum, four of which proved fatal. About fifty of the boys were attacked with the disease, but Father Croke reports that all the patients are now convalescent, and the general health at the Asylum is now first rate. This is the first serious illness that has ever occurred among the great army of lads and there is no apparent cause for it."*

The boys who died in 1883 were: John Butterly, aged 13 on March 17; Walter O'Brien, aged 13 on May 23; John Raga, aged 10 on July 13; John Malloy, aged 13 on July 11; Eugene Silver, aged 11 on August 11. The last three certainly were from the epidemic.

In the month of August the Honorable J. J. Ayers, State Printer, and Mr. Moreland, Private Secretary to the Governor and Secretary of the Board of Examiners, visited St. Vincent's on a regular inspection tour of the orphanages of the state and spoke highly of the condition in which they found the place.

March 3, 1884 stands as a very important date in the life of St. Vincent's and St. Raphael's Church in San Rafael. On that day the Archbishop[9] separated St. Vincent's from the parish and appointed Rev. Hugh Lagan the first resident pastor of San Rafael. One month later, on April 1, he moved Father Lynch and sent Father John Vallentini as assistant to Father Croke. With this lifting of the responsibility for the parish, Father Croke's burden was light-

The infirmary cottage, located in the front on the north side.

The interior of the infirmary cottage.

ened. The care of over 500 boys for 24 hours a day was indeed sufficient to tax anyone's strength and ability. It had been almost ten years since the local paper had suggested a resident pastor in San Rafael. When it did occur, Father Lagan certainly was the right choice.

Before omitting the parish from our story it seems proper to say at least what Father Lagan accomplished in his first year. Naturally Father Croke had not been able to devote the time or effort to St. Raphael's that would have been ideal. Therefore Father Lagan found much to improve right from the start. On July 17, 1884 the following article appeared:

> "The Catholic Church on 5th St. has one of the finest situations in San Rafael but for a long time it has apparently been neglected. Last summer saw a change for the better, the old church building was repainted and fitted up for a school which is in successful operation; fences were repaired; walks cleaned up; and put on a new appearance of hope for the future. Since Father Lagan has been appointed Pastor many things have been done and more will be done to put it in proper order. The old picket fence on Fifth street has been taken away, and the whole frontage, some 350 feet, planted with cypress trees for a hedge, and a four wire fence with neat posts and gates replaces the old one. The old cemetery to the right of the church is being cleared of the wild bushes and trees. The bodies there interred are to be taken up and buried in the new cemetery, and it is the intention of Father to have built a pastoral residence where he can receive his parishioners this fall. The Church has been neatly carpeted, the interior painted and other improvements made. Mass is said on Sundays at 8:00 and 10:30."

Father Lagan worked rapidly. He organized the parish for a fair which was held in October and which netted $8,071.45. On December 11, 1884 the paper carried the following description of his activities:

> "Extensive changes are going on at the Catholic Church property. The Church building is being overhauled by Adam Murphy both inside and out. The interior is being beautifully paneled, two magnificent altars are being added and the entire exterior is assuming a new and ornamental appearance. A new and higher bell tower is to be built. Nearly all the bodies have been removed from the old cemetery and already the foundations of a grand parsonage, 35 x 75 and to contain sixteen rooms, are being laid therein."

On Monday February 23, 1885 the carpenters commenced their work on the new Rectory. One month later Father Lagan[10] moved the old church which had been converted into a school, to a new location and announced that it would be renovated and used as a hall for meetings. By April 23, 1885, everything was in readiness for a solemn dedication on which occasion Archbishop Riordan[11] blessed the newly remodeled plant. The total cost of Father Lagan's year of work was $24,000.

Meanwhile it seems to have been too much for Father Croke to see all this building going on, for he too had to build something. What he built we do not know. Certainly it was not as extensive as his efforts in the '70s, but the following article appeared on Thursday, May 28, 1885:

> "Archbishop Riordan administered the rite of Confirmation to some 200 lads at the Orphan Asylum last Monday and also to a class of misses from the neighborhood. At the same time he dedicated the new buildings recently completed. Many guests and friends of the Asylum were present, and they all concurred heartily in the Archbishop's commendation of Father Croke's management of this great trust. He said there were plenty of men who would like to be Bishops, but if he had to fill Father Croke's place, he would not know where to find the man. There are over 500 boys; one dormitory building is over 300 feet long; every day's baking of bread takes two barrels of flour; there is not a case of sickness and all the attendants are neat, systematic and thrifty."

On August 27, 1885, the Archbishop moved Father John Vallentini to San Rafael. There does not seem to have been anyone to assist Father Croke immediately as this decade of years comes to a close and St. Vincent's approached its thirty-third year of life.

CHAPTER IX

THE BOYS OF '82 AND
LIFE IN '88

It is time now to pause in our narrative and take a look inside St. Vincent's. Our first point of consideration should be the children themselves. Because of the set up in State aid, excellent books were kept by Father Croke, and between 1880 and 1888 he also recorded the placement of older boys when they left St. Vincent's. Also during these same years he published quarterly the list of new-comers, giving their condition — orphans or half-orphans — their names, ages, and dates of admission. A summary of this record of admissions which, of course, was the cause of all the building expansion, is as follows:

Number of children admitted to St. Vincent's during the Quarter ending:

	Father dead	Mother dead	Whole orphans	Both parents living	Total
March 31, 1882	25	19	3	9	56
June 30, 1882	6	8	14	7	35
Sept. 30, 1882	18	16	5	13	52
Dec. 31, 1882	19	21	13	14	67
March 31, 1883	14	15	6	17	52
June 30, 1883	17	10	6	9	42
March 31, 1884	11	28	15	24	78
June 30, 1884	10	24	1	9	44
Sept. 30, 1884	16	12	16	8	52

No wonder the Catholic Directories for these years show an enormous population:

1882: 516 boys   *1883: 540 boys*   *1884: 554 boys*

This last figure seems to be the all time high.

For the moment we turn our attention to the year 1882. By this time State aid was given semi-annually rather than quarterly, and the amount had been raised by the State to $100 per year for whole orphans and $75 a year for half orphans. Boys became ineligible for State aid once they became fourteen.

Among the eligible boys, the longest in residence at St. Vincent's was John Ryan who had come on July 21, 1871 at the age of two. The next oldest eligible resident was James Blaney, who had been admitted on January 22, 1872, at the age of three. Next oldest was Robert Morrison, who came on July 18, 1872 at the age of four. The list continues with the name of Michael Cunningham as the only eligible one still in the institution who had come in 1874. There were seven who had come in 1875 at the age of six. They were: John Donohoe, Robert Browne, Joseph Renner, William Jacobs, Henry Gough, George Macklin, Edward Hynes, and Daniel McVanner. If any of them are alive today they would be eighty-six years old.

The Register also records the boys who left St. Vincent's during the half year ending June 30, 1882. Only sixty-seven boys left during this six months period, whereas the record given above shows that ninety-two were admitted. No wonder the number constantly climbed. However, the record also shows that this flux in population was a regular thing. It is often felt that children sent to an institution such as St. Vincent's were just left there and kept for years and years. The following chart showing the state of affairs as of June 30, 1882 demonstrates that the average stay was for four years. The classification is the one used in the Record.
Boys still at St. Vincent's on June 30, 1882:

Year admitted	Whole orphans	Half orphans	Abandoned children
1871	—	1	—
1872	2	3	—
1873	—	1	—
1874	1	—	1
1875	5	8	—
1876	4	14	—
1877	12	28	4
1878	13	33	3
1879	27	67	13
1880	25	58	16
1881	17	96	10
1882	15	64	21

Perhaps still more interesting is a partial list of the children who left St. Vincent's during the half year ending June 30, 1882, given in Chart I.

The most interesting group of all consists of those boys who were over fourteen and were still present at St. Vincent's on June 30, 1882, These were followed through in the Record and their length of stay recorded, as well as their eventual placement as given in Chart II.

For a glimpse of life in St. Vincent's we must turn to the year 1888, for in that year the secretary for the Board of Examiners was Mr. S. P. Maslin, who gave a very thorough inspection and who left us abundant evidence of life as he found it.

The boys arose at 6:00 A.M. In winter time this meant darkness, save for kerosene lamps, and no heat. After arising they washed thoroughly. This too was in cold water, but in this they differed in no manner from the general population. Hot water was still a luxury; to obtain it meant heating it on a stove or in a boiler. Breakfast consisted of coffee and bread with a little milk in the coffee. School commenced at 9:00 A.M. There was a fifteen minute recess at 10 o'clock. The main meal of the day was at noon. It consisted usually of soup, meat, potatoes, and bread. The noon recreation lasted for an hour and a half. Then school reconvened until a recess at 3:00 P.M. The classes then resumed until 4:30. Supper was served at 6:00 P.M., consisting of tea and bread. The boys went to bed at 7:30. We notice in the diet an absence of milk and butter. Strange as it may seem, Father Croke never increased the dairy. There were forty cows when Father Birmingham left, certainly sufficient to supply the needs of 280 boys. But now with 500, there were still only forty cows. Butter was served on fast days, such as Fridays, when there was no meat. Pies were the main delicacy served on feast days and holidays. This simple diet evidently proved a healthy one, for the excellent health of the children was always a matter for comment by visitors, official or casual.

The greatest problem in those years seems to have been cleanliness, both of the institution and of the boys. Always, the visitor, the inspector, the reporter, everyone commented on the immaculate cleanliness of the huge dormitories and the bedding, because this department was in the care of the Dominican Sisters. Of the other departments, the state of cleanliness depended upon the individual employee who happened to occupy the position at that time. As for the boys themselves, everyone knows how hard it is to keep a boy clean. To do it for 500 was almost a superhuman task. The job was made doubly difficult because of several factors. First, nothing was paved. The play yard had a hard dirt surface; all walks connecting various buildings were unpaved. Secondly, the problem of bathing was tremendous. Showers were non-existent in those days. All bathing had to be in bath tubs. To give 500 boys a shower would be an enormous task. What must it have been to try to give them a bath? The water had to be heated in a boiler, for which a special fire had to be kept going all day. The bath room was small and the tubs shallow and narrow. In the winter time there was no way to heat the bath room, therefore, the boys were not a bit anxious to bathe. Luckily, in the summer there was swimming in the creek, a natural means of keeping clean. Added to this was the fact that the bath tubs were kept busy taking care of the new arrivals. One would have to see in order to believe the frightful condition in which many of the newcomers arrived. Poverty unfortunately is often mixed up with dirt, although there is no real affinity. The Sisters often commented on the work involved in receiving a new boy. He had to be carefully bathed, the lice removed, his clothing burned, new clothing issued, and his sores treated.

The task of keeping the clothing in repair and clean was also another major undertaking. In 1888, this was the task of Sister M. Catherine, who had been at St. Vincent's for five years. She had a double job. She attended the dining room, where she watched over the washing of dishes and tables. Between meals her assignment was the sewing room. Here, with one assistant, Miss Cecelia Farley, a seamstress who had been at St. Vincent's a year and a half, Sister Catherine was in charge of supplying and mending the boys' clothing. Miss Farley mended clothes three days of the week; she made shirts and waists two days. Her average production of new shirts per week was twenty-four. She made them of flannel, plaids, ginghams, merinos, and flour sacks. Also at certain times Sister Catherine and Miss Farley made sheets and pillow cases. They were assisted at times by Sister M. Paul, who had been at St. Vincent's for ten years. She also had charge of one of the huge dormitories, and the wash room. One of her main tasks was the filling of mattresses. After all, Simmons and Sealy were not doing big business in 1888. Sister M. Paul made her own mattresses. She filled them either with dried straw (tule) or with hair. Since the dormitories had between 150 and 200 beds, Sister's task was indeed great. Sister

Margaret, also at St. Vincent's five years, had charge of another dormitory. But in addition, she had the care of the clothes room. It was her task to mark, sort, and distribute the clean and new clothing for the boys. Besides, she was the Infirmarian. Daily she cared for the cuts, the sores, the colds, and watched over the patients, who usually averaged about ten. The fourth Sister doing domestic work was Sister M. Pius, who had been one year at St. Vincent's. Her job was the kitchen and the storeroom.

The supply of meat alone gives some idea of the quantities involved in feeding over 500 boys. Most of the meat was bought from W. N. Anderson's Market in San Rafael. The official record of the six months ending May 1, 1888 shows that St. Vincent's bought, in that period, 37,261 pounds of beef and mutton. The record shows the amounts distributed as follows:

November 1887	. . .	6002 pounds
December 1887	. . .	6484 pounds
January 1888	. . .	5511 pounds
February 1888	. . .	6265 pounds
March 1888	. . .	6423 pounds
April 1888	. . .	6576 pounds

In addition to this, the meat slaughtered on St. Vincent's farm amounted to 3,216 pounds plus 460 pounds of turkey. The total amount for the six months was 40,937 pounds, which averages 1,550 pounds a month or 284½ pounds a day, leaving out Friday.

Sister M. Pius also supervised the cook, who in May, 1888 was new, a native of Luxemburg, Henry Budding by name. All the cleaning and other work was done by the boys. Sister M. Pius also issued the supplies to the baker, Matthew Hollywood, who had been two years at St. Vincent's. Since this gentleman baked all the bread and pies, he required four and a half barrels of flour per day. The yeast he made from potatoes, hops, and malt. He had one older boy who helped him. Shoes for five hundred boys! Even the thought is sufficient to repel one. Yet Father Croke solved this problem by employing a shoemaker, Samuel Cupid, who had been at St. Vincent's for several years. This skilled workman mended between eighteen and twenty-five pairs of shoes each week. He had one boy aged fourteen to help him. Again, we must remember that all the work was done by hand. There was no modern shoe repair machinery to help. One other employee of eight years held a fairly responsible position. He was Philip Doland, in charge of the dairy. Five of the boys helped him in the milking of the cows. In 1888, the boys who worked with him were Eddy Lane, aged seventeen, Joe Wiler and Joseph Hall. The other two were still young enough to go to school. On the farm were William Dwyer, employed one year, and Michael Williams, who had five years service to the school. The engineer was William O'Dell. This was the staff in 1888.

The Shoe Shop in the Old Days.

The Laundry.

CHAPTER X

DISASTER STRIKES
MAY, 1888

On May 19, 1888, the routine Saturday chores were in the process of being accomplished. Father Croke was in Petaluma on a visit. About 10:30 A.M. Sister M. Agatha, the Superior, was in the sacristy of the Chapel fixing a bouquet of flowers for Sunday Mass. Suddenly a boy burst into the sacristy shouting, "FIRE— Sister, there's a fire!"

Sister Agatha flew from the sacristy; the Chapel bell began to call the neighbors; Sisters and lay help ran out from every department. The sight that met their eyes must have struck terror into their hearts. The old wooden buildings were on fire. The old Chapel in the northwest corner was a mass of flames. Someone ran to the telephone and called the Fire Department in San Rafael. There the citizens in alarm responded generously. The two fire horses, Jewell and Murray, were hooked up and started the long five miles to St. Vincent's. Meanwhile, someone had to start fighting the fire. The Sisters, teachers and neighbors pitched in. Their first task was to tear down the high board fence that connected the main building with the old Chapel and the clothes room adjoining. The men arrived from Miller Hall across the road and from St. Vincent's own farm. They organized a bucket brigade and passed water to the roof of the adjoining dormitory building which they kept well watered. It was impossible to save the burning buildings.

Meanwhile, Father Rheinhart, worried about the boys and the possibility of the fire spreading and trapping them, opened the gate in the high board fence that surrounded the property and told the boys to scatter to the nearby hills and watch from there. Sister Agatha, also in fear that the fire would spread, thought of the records and ledgers in Father Croke's room. She left the scene of the fire and hurrying to the Director's quarters found the door locked, as expected. Taking a mop, she smashed the glass, opened the window, and went in. Then she gathered up the books and handing them to two boys, left in as great a hurry as she had arrived.

Mr. Miller's daughters drove in from across the road and told the Sisters that their father, the beloved gentleman who had befriended St. Vincent's since the day of its foundation, was sitting at home weeping bitterly. These girls then joined with the Sisters in the fire prevention work.

The Chapel, the clothes room and the pavilion were all a mass of flames. Luckily, the wind was away from the main building. Quickly the dried wood burned and especially since there was no water to put out the fire. What was available was being used to prevent the fire from spreading.

By the time the San Rafael Fire Department reached the premises, the buildings were almost gone. For two hours these men and the neighbors worked to prevent the fire from destroying the whole institution. Eventually they won the victory. The rest of St. Vincent's was saved; the fire was under control.

Only then did anyone have time to take notice of the boys or to ask questions or estimate the damage. The value of the burned buildings was figured at $5,000. About 50,000 feet of lumber had been burned. Then the news slowly leaked out that the fire was of incendiary origin. One of the boys had set it. On the previous night he had broken a coal oil lamp and saturated paper with the coal oil. Using this he had set the fire in the old Chapel on Saturday morning. Then it was discovered that this particular boy and many others were missing. Taking advantage of the freedom given them by Father Rheinhart, they had gone off in every direction. Over 200 were missing at 3 o'clock. Slowly they began to be rounded up and brought back. That same evening seventy-five boys were picked up in San Rafael and were sent home like cattle in a box car. By evening, the whereabouts of sixty-three were still unknown. One boy almost lost his life. He evidently started toward the bay. But he got stuck in the marsh lands as the tide began to come in. Slowly his legs sank deeper and deeper into the gray clay. The more he struggled the deeper he sank. Inextricably caught, the water soon reached his waist; then as the tide came in, it climbed to his arms. By the time a man rescued him in a boat, the water was within two inches of the boy's mouth.

Word of the disaster reached Father Croke in Petaluma. Like all such news, the first word he received was that the whole place had burned down. About halfway home he received a report that only half of the buildings had burned. As he came down the hill and sighted the cross atop the Chapel spire he knew that the latter rumor was more likely correct. He reached St. Vincent's by 11 o'clock that night. But shock was to prove too much for Father Croke. Broken in health by his long, hard years, it took just this disaster to shake him seriously. He stayed only a few days and then left for a long vacation. Actually his departure was of a permanent nature.

Father Croke left on a trip on July 25, 1888. He went by train to his old Diocese, visiting in Portland and Vancouver Island for several days. Then he took the train heading east. In a letter he remarked how the journey followed almost the same route he had covered on horseback so many years before. He reached the East coast in the fall and visited there for some time. It was obvious however that his condition was poor. He entered St. Vincent's Hospital in New York City at the end of the year. On January 7, 1889, a telegram was received saying that Father Croke was dead. For thirteen years he had guided the destinies of St. Vincent's. Now he was no longer its Father. The children given to his care would never see him again. Some of them had caused his death by their thoughtlessness. He had left their midst with a heavy heart. He was not to come home to them even in death. His funeral took place in St. Joseph's Church, New York City, on Wednesday, January 9, 1889. Archbishop Corrigan of New York and three other Bishops were among those who were present at the Solemn Requiem Mass. The remains were sent to San Francisco by train, and on Saturday, January 31, were interred in Calvary Cemetery.

One month later, a Solemn Mass was sung at St. Vincent's. It was the Month's Mind Mass on February 7th. Father Hugh Lagan, pastor of San Rafael, was the Celebrant. Father J. A. Cassidy of St. Paul's in San Francisco and Father M. O. Riordan of Menlo Park were the Deacon and the Subdeacon.

Immediately after the fire the Archbishop sent Father P. Scanlan to restore order to St. Vincent's. Witnesses testified that the excitement caused by the fire made school almost an impossibility. The loss of the clothes room created a difficulty for one thing. The loss of Mr. Jeremiah Whalen, the Principal of the school, was another disturbing factor. Thus, at one time St. Vincent's lost its Director and its Principal. Needless to say, the troublesome element took advantage of the situation. Thus it was some weeks before Father Scanlan had affairs back to normal.

The school at this time consisted of six classes, four taught by laymen and two taught by Sisters. The Sisters had been teaching only since August 1, 1885, when Sister Agatha and Sister Ursula had been sent for this purpose. In the spring of 1888 Sister Ursula had been replaced by Sister Eulalia.

Thus in May, 1888 the classes were divided as follows: Mr. Jeremiah Whalen, the Principal for the past ten years, taught the upper class of oldest boys. John J. Croke, the brother of Father Croke, had for nine years what was known as the Fourth Reader class, a group of sixty-seven boys all about nine years of age. Henry O'Reilly, who had been at St. Vincent's for two years taught a class of sixty-six boys. John B. Dewing, a native of Switzerland, at St. Vincent's over two years, taught sixty-five boys ranging in age from nine to twelve. The Sisters taught the smaller boys, Sister Eulalia's class being composed of sixty-eight boys, ages seven to nine. Sister handled them by dividing her flock into four groups according to their proficiency. The First Reader class was in the care of Sister Agatha, the Superior.

We see in the fire and the consequent disturbance the mistakes made by Father Croke coming to full fruition. In matters of external affairs he had certainly proven his genius. The tremendous expansion in buildings and the consequent financial problems were readily solved by him. But in the internal affairs his foresight was limited. For one thing, his generous heart never knew when to say stop. Evidently he took everyone who applied. The end result was twofold: too many boys, and an undesirable element among them. Over 500 boys was definitely too many particularly considering the size of the staff. Obviously, these boys were not too difficult to handle because most of them being half-orphans had at least one interested parent to shower love, attention, and interest on their boys. Also the children of 1888 still had a great respect for authority, something missing in our modern generation as a whole. These two factors made the task of the staff in 1888 much less formidable than the numbers would lead us to think.

The second difficulty was the disturbed element that was taken in. Since Father Croke took everyone, naturally some undesirables were passed on to him. In the words of Henry O'Reilly, the teacher:

"Some of the boys are sent here when their parents cannot control them. Some new arrivals are graduates of the Police Courts and have always been subjected to contaminating influences. I understand that most people of the Catholic religion believe that if they will send boys here, there is such restraint that they will be immediately bettered in morals and condition. But, owing to the number we have to deal with, such measures take a great deal of time for their accomplishment."

Unfortunately, Mr. O'Reilly's comment on the opinion of the people was true and was to remain true for many years. Because St. Vincent's opened its doors to the undesirable as well as to the orphan, the word would get around that it was a school for bad boys, a kind of Catholic reformatory. This was never true. But because Father Croke and some of his successors did assist the juvenile authorities of San Francisco and Marin by taking many of their charges, this minor element in the house would cause the disturbances and receive the attention and publicity that would stigmatize the whole institution. It was not until 1922 that a definite policy was established that no more problem boys of any kind would be accepted at St. Vincent's. Rather than being a stigma on the institution, it should be one of its proud boasts, that when there were no other institutions to care for these disturbed youths, St. Vincent's pioneered in this field of social work.

The Lower Play Yard in the 1900's.

Father William D. McKinnon, Sixth Director of St. Vincent's—1888-1893.

CHAPTER XI

A NEW LEASE ON LIFE
1888 - 1892

With the retirement of Father Croke, the Archbishop was faced with the problem he had openly admitted that he dreaded, namely the appointment of a successor to Father Croke. Father Scanlon's appointment had been only temporary. Eventually, by the end of June, the Archbishop appointed his own Secretary as the new Director of St. Vincent's. He was Father William D. McKinnon, a man thirty years of age but only one year a priest.

Born in Melrose, Prince Edward Island, on August 1, 1858, William McKinnon came to San Francisco in 1875 when he was seventeen years old. His purpose in coming was far from any idea of studying for the priesthood. Evidently at that time he had no such thoughts. He came to work for his uncle who had a partnership in a lumber company. It was not until 1880 that he even had any thought about completing his education. Finally in that year he enrolled at Santa Clara University and took a commercial course, evidently to benefit himself in the business world. Perhaps it was the direct contact with the Jesuit Fathers in the University that first set his mind thinking along the lines of the priesthood. Whatever was the cause, the following year he started his classical studies in order to prepare himself for the seminary. In 1882 he went to the Junior Seminary in Ottawa, Canada and two years later came back to San Francisco to attend the Archdiocesan Seminary which was then located at Mission San Jose. This small Seminary was at the time suffering from a lack of students. When in 1885 four were ordained, the Seminary closed its doors. The remaining students were transferred to St. Mary's Seminary in Baltimore, Maryland, and among them was William McKinnon. After two years at Baltimore he was ordained a priest.

His first appointment on his return was to St. Brigid's Church. His Pastor at that time was none other than Father Peter Birmingham, the former Director of St. Vincent's. Perhaps Father McKinnon often heard tales from his Pastor of the early days of St. Vincent's. His stay at St. Brigid's was for only five months for on January 18, 1888, he was appointed Secretary to Archbishop Riordan. This was the post he held at the time of his transfer to St. Vincent's in June of that same year.

Upon his arrival, Father McKinnon at once manifested "rare executive ability" in the words of Mr. Maslin of the State Board of Examiners. Father McKinnon at once hired more help. We read in the Archives of the Dominican Sisters for June 5, 1888 that upon the request of the Archbishop that more Sisters be sent to teach the boys at the orphan asylum, it was agreed to send several. His next improvement was to concrete many places where there had still been an earthen floor, for instance in the bakery, the meat house and the outside walks. He had torn down the old lavatories and built new ones, and improved the drainage system. His best achievement was the division of the larger boys from the smaller ones by the separation of play yards.

Within three months after his arrival, the Editor of the Marin Journal, affected with curiosity, as he openly admits, sent a reporter to visit the institution. His description tells best what Father McKinnon accomplished.

> "We are happy to state that everything appeared neat and comfortable. There are at present 429 boys of all ages up to nineteen years in the asylum. The dormitories are light and fully ventilated by numerous windows on three sides of the room. The beds looked clean and each one was provided with a sheet, blanket, coverlid and pillow. The long tables were set in the dining room, and from the enumeration of the articles furnished the boys at meals, it was evident that the kinds of food were wholesome and in as great abundance and variety as the resources of the asylum would allow.
>
> The bathrooms were visited next — large rectangular rooms with continuous bath tubs extending around the walls and about a square in the center of the apartment. The tubs were being filled in anticipation of the rush of a squad of 40 boys as soon as the school exercises should close. An officer stands at the door of the bathroom and takes the numbers of the scholars as they enter, and in this way, the certainty of every boy having his weekly or semi-weekly scrub is assured.
>
> The boys whom we did see on the grounds looked in good condition, and were dressed as well as most farmer's children; in fact, better than many of them. A neat uniform, consisting of a grey mixed blouse belted in at the waist, with blue shoulder straps on which is displayed in metal figures the boy's school number; pants of the same cloth and a peaked cap to match will be adopted as soon as enough suits are finished

to clothe the entire school. And military drill with wooden muskets has already been instituted, greatly to the delight of the boys."

With this report we get our first glimpse into the military tendencies in Father McKinnon. The drilling with muskets, the uniform, the numbers, all these manifest a tendency toward the military which would blossom forth into the heroic Chaplain McKinnon which phase of his priestly career has made him famous. Meanwhile, today we evaluate these steps taken by Father McKinnon in a different manner from his contemporaries. Anything which impersonalizes a child or makes him just a number is frowned upon in our modern child care institutions. However at St. Vincent's as Father McKinnon found it in 1888, the system had its own good effects.

To assist him in his work, Father McKinnon had the help of Father William Brennan. This priest too made constructive efforts on behalf of the boys. He took over the singing and strove to build up a vested choir which rendered itself proud on many future occasions. In October, 1888, both priests were called upon to try to bring consolation to their friend James Miller, their neighbor and friend across the road. The occasion was the accidental death of Mr. Miller's second son, Martin Van Buren Miller. A man forty-five years of age, and a State Prison Director living in Martinez, he had been killed by a train. This new blow to the aged James Miller was to hasten his own death.

At the end of 1888, Father McKinnon, like his predecessor, commenced to build. The building he erected was the most pretentious of all. An article in the Marin Journal on February 14, 1889, gives a fine description.

"A large addition has just been completed at St. Vincent's Orphan Asylum. It consists of a structure running across the east end (where the swimming pool is now) and connecting the two divisions of the old building. The new part is about 40 by 137 feet, three stories high, each story having twelve foot porches. It has completely changed the appearence of the place from the railroad, toward which the front is, beautiful in design and finish. Additional porches have been constructed on the old wings of the building, giving much more room for open air recreation and every way improving the place. Mr. C. Chisolm was the builder, and his work is very thorough. The addition cost $24,000. J. A. West is now painting the Asylum and it is a big job."

The "new" wing erected by Father McKinnon in 1889.

Father McKinnon's new wing from the inside courtyard on an exhibition day.

Another description of the new building tells the use for which each floor was destined. "The lower floor is for a gymnasium, recreation hall and library. The second story is devoted to classrooms and an exhibition hall for plays, entertainments, etc., while the third is reserved for a dormitory."

Evidently with the building of this new dormitory, Father McKinnon discontinued the use of the second floor of the Administration wing as a dormitory. Instead he had it divided up into rooms and moved his own quarters into it. It was also under his supervision that the dairy buildings, chicken houses and sheds were further removed from the main buildings than they had been previously. His general attention to the farm resulted in the planting of orchards. An article in the local paper on April 11, 1889, refers to this activity as follows: "Several thousand fruit trees have been planted on the grounds of St. Vincent's Orphan Asylum, which will soon yield nearly a full supply for the wants of the institution." Other references to Father McKinnon's orchards tell us that they included olive trees, an orange grove, and even a vineyard, and that the grounds had been beautified by the planting of English laurels, horse-chestnuts, acacias and pepper trees.

Perhaps his greatest achievement from our modern point of view was the introduction of technical training for the older boys. The boys were taught sufficient farming to be able to set the trees and vines in the new orchards. Many of them were given plots of land to cultivate and Father McKinnon held out prizes to reward them for their efforts. A tailor shop, a shoe shop, and a carpentry shop were set up for the older boys to learn the trades. On one Saturday in April, 1889, thirty-nine new pairs of shoes were delivered from the shoe shop, the result of a week's work in that department. Another introduction, one not destined to benefit the institution financially, was the start of harness making. In the harness shop the boys made sets of harness for sale. Unfortunately, the market was not in demand of harnesses at that time and the venture was doomed to failure.

Still other improvements attempted by Father McKinnon included the enlarging of the dairy farm. By April, 1890 it was reported that there were one hundred and sixty-five head of cattle on the farm and sufficient milk and butter available for all the boys. At the same time Father McKinnon invested in a new means of lighting the institution, namely, gas lighting. Fixtures and necessary piping were installed throughout the buildings. At the same time too, he had men engaged in digging in the hills in search of further water supplies.

On Sunday, April 27, 1890, St. Vincent's was host to some 300 men who came to attend the quarterly meeting of the St. Vincent de Paul Society. Archbishop Riordan was present to greet the arrivals. The guests had taken the 8:00 A.M. ferry from San Francisco to Tiburon and then the train to St. Vincent's. As soon as they arrived they went to the Chapel where Father Cottle offered Mass for them and Father Brennan's Boys Choir sang the music of the Mass. The Archbishop preached the sermon and then the delegates held their meeting. When the meeting ended all adjourned to the new building to be entertained by the boys; the description of what took place is as follows:

> "When all the visitors were seated, 100 boys, all neatly dressed, marched on to the stage and sang a chorus of welcome. After that a lad about 14 years old came out and delivered an address in fine style. He was heartily applauded on its conclusion. The address was followed by a kindergarten song in which the boys illustrated a lad trying to make up his mind which trade he would follow. Then came a recitation. A flag drill followed which was particularly good, and when the lads crossed their flags and sang 'Star Spangled Banner', they brought down the house. 'A Father's Visit to his Sons' was next recited, and then two of the boys sang the A B C duet in such a manner as to win a hearty recall. A chorus by the whole school brought the entertainment to a close. Great praise is due to Miss M. McCue, Miss L. McKinnon and Miss A. Byers who trained the children. The accompaniments were played in an artistic manner by Miss McKinnon and Miss McCue."

It was at the close of these exercises that the Archbishop told the assembled group that the improvements made in the two years of Father McKinnon's incumbency had cost $50,000. This can be readily understood when we realize that half that amount went into the new building, and the other half into the planting of trees, installation of gas, setting up of equipment for shops, increase of the number of help and consequent salaries, and the painting of all the buildings.

It was on the occasion of this visit by the St. Vincent de Paul Society that an article in the Monitor appeared telling something about the Alumni of St. Vincent's. It read as follows:

"Since St. Vincent's first opened, nearly 5,000 boys have found a shelter beneath its roof. While all of these have not turned out well, St. Vincent's has sent out boys who have reached high positions in every walk of life. They are honored members of the bar, of the medical profession and of the ministry, and have found their way into legislative halls of their State. Two of the most prominent members of the last (1889) Legislature were boys educated at St. Vincent's. A leading writer on the New York Herald was a former inmate of this institution, while prosperous fruit growers in this and other counties as well as successful business men all over the State owe their education to the same school."

Two deaths occurred in 1890 which had an effect on St. Vincent's. One was that of James Mervyn Donahue, aged thirty-one, the son of the late Col. Peter Donahue, the builder and founder of the railroad. When Mr. Donahue's will was filed for probate in March, 1890, it was found that he had left a legacy of $20,000 to St. Vincent's. Had this legacy been received, it would have been a great boon to Father McKinnon; but there were other things in the will which caused it to be contested and litigation was still going on five years later. The other death was that of James Miller, the old pioneer and faithful friend and neighbor. After a long illness, he died on Tuesday, November 25, 1890 in the seventy-ninth year of his life. His funeral naturally was from St. Vincent's Chapel of the Most Holy Rosary at 10:00 on Friday, November 29, 1890. The Solemn Requiem Mass, presided over by Archbishop Riordan, was sung by Father J. Cleary of Petaluma who was a relative. The deacon and subdeacon were both former assistants of St. Vincent's, Father M. O. Riordan of Menlo Park, and Father P. R. Lynch of St. James in San Francisco. Father McKinnon preached the funeral sermon. Parts of the Mass were sung by the boys together with an adult choir from San Francisco. Over twenty priests were present in the Chapel for this funeral of the foster father of St. Vincent's

The year 1891 was to witness a further change in St. Vincent's, not in the buildings, the staff or the boys, but in the farm. It was to take the form of a new and entirely different enterprise. An article on September 3, 1891 in the Marin Journal best describes it:

"Father McKinnon, who is in charge of the Asylum is quite an enthusiastic horseman, and strange to say, although he never attended a horse race until the present Petaluma meeting, he has purchased a number of first class stallions and brood mares with which he intends to stock the 2,500 acres of rich land. The former Superintendents of the institution devoted their attention to the production of cattle, but the business

did not pay, and when Father McKinnon went into control he sold out
the herds and is now replacing them with royally bred standard trotters.
Among the stallions he has is a handsome black three year old that he
purchased at the late Holly sale for $600. The horse is a splendid indi-
vidual and now shows quarters at 35 seconds and has trotted a mile with
a little handling in 2.28.

  Another good one of the farm is the well known brood mare Ver-
onica. It will be remembered that Gilbert Tompkins bought the mare
at the Skinner sale for $2,500. She was bought at auction by St. Vincent's
for $1,400. Since that time, Mr. Tompkins has paid Father McKinnon
$1,100 for a colt she has had."

On February 4, 1892, it was reported that Father McKinnon
had sold in the previous week $1,450 worth of colts from his stock
farm.

Interesting as it was, the horse raising business was a risky one,
and instead of being a source of profit it became another liability.
The debt which had been $50,000 in May of 1890 was now around
$90,000. The harness making venture was a financial loss. The fruit
trees were a loss, as it seems that most of them prospered only the
first year or two and then died. Meanwhile Father McKinnon was
unable to raise any funds from any other source. The Archbishop
became worried about the debt. The only solution he could see
was to move Father McKinnon and put in a more economically
minded man. Thus on February 6, 1898, Father McKinnon[12] was
moved from St. Vincent's and appointed temporarily as Pastor of
San Pablo. Three weeks later he was transferred to Rio Vista. Thus
St. Vincent's lost the most colorful of its Directors and the boys
lost an understanding friend. But their loss was to become someone else's gain.

CHAPTER XII

A CHANGE IS IN THE AIR

On the retirement of Father Croke in 1888, the Archbishop felt that it would be best for St. Vincent's if a religious community could take over the place in its entirety, not only teaching in the school but also taking care of the administration. He had appealed to the Christian Brothers, but they were unable to supply sufficient Brothers at that time. Now with the transfer of Father McKinnon, Archbishop Riordan tried again. This time it looked more hopeful but the Brothers could not accept the undertaking at once. The Archbishop would have to appoint a temporary administrator. His selection fell on Father Dennis O. Crowley who already had a full time job as Director of the Youths Directory. Having proven himself a successful administrator, he certainly was the one to put St. Vincent's back on its feet economically.

Born in Castleton, County Cork in 1852, Dennis Crowley came to America at the age of nineteen. He served two years as an apprentice in the printing trade before deciding to come west. Then setting his eyes on the Comstock Lode, he traveled to Virginia City, Nevada, where he worked for a time as a miner and later as a time keeper at the Ophir Mine. Out of the savinge accumulated, he paid his way to St. Vincent's College in Los Angeles and later transferred to St. Charles College, a Junior Seminary, in Ellicot City, Maryland. His studies in theology were made at St. Mary's Seminary, Baltimore, Maryland, where he was ordained a priest on December 22, 1883. For a year he served in the East, but in 1884 he was called home by the Archbishop and was appointed as Assistant at St. Anthony's Church, Oakland. One year later the Archbishop appointed him as Pastor of Dixon, a parish comprising the towns of Dixon and Vacaville where he served for two years. However the heart of Father Crowley was in a special kind of work. He appealed to the Archbishop to allow him to do something for the neglected and abandoned boys that he had seen roaming the streets of San Francisco. Father Crowley, having been a printer's apprentice and a miner, knew the value of a trade for growing boys. The home he proposed to establish would emphasize this type of training. With the permission of the Archbishop the Youths Directory was established in February, 1887. Father Crowley purchased a site on Howard Street near 17th Street, and erected a four story building. It was to this successful administrator and Father of Boys that the Archbishop turned and asked him to straighten out St. Vincent's finances until the Christian Brothers would be able to take over. Father Crowley's appointment to St. Vincent's was on January 22, 1893.

He himself states in a subsequent letter to the Archbishop that there were 474 boys at St. Vincent's on the day he took charge. "Of that number 120 were over fourteen years of age, most of these over sixteen." This seems quite a change from the previous custom of "farming out" the boys once they were fourteen. But Father McKinnon had tried a new experiment. The trades he attempted to have taught and the farm work with the horses called for older boys. Thus he had held on to them. But, we recall, a boy over fourteen was ineligible for state aid. Therefore there was no income to support these 120 boys. This was one of the financial drains that Father Crowley had to correct. Six months later in June, 1893, he was able to report to the Archbishop:

> *"Places have been procured for all the boys who have passed the legal age, three being employed in the Asylum. In sending them out, we did not laud them to the skies, but told the parties plainly what we knew about the lads. In this way the people were not deceived and all these boys, with three exceptions, are doing fairly well. I found in the Youths Directory that it was better for the boys, for the persons taking him, and for the reputation of the House to tell the whole truth about any boy whose character was under discussion prior to his being taken into a family."*

Father Crowley then states that with the removal of the older boys it was much easier to manage the younger children.

> *"For this new order of things, we are very much indebted to the Youths Directory. It is not only a feeder for the Asylum but also a safety valve. Whenever I have a 'hard case' here who was causing trouble and leavening the whole mass with his viciousness, I took him over to 2030 Howard St., leaving the impression behind that he was booked for Whittier. This plan has worked admirably, the idea acts as a deterent and the well-disposed boys are easily ruled by kindness. Meanwhile, finding no confederates in the Directory, the boys cool down and in a week or two he is farmed out to Marysville, Tulare City or elsewhere."*

Thus Father Crowley tells how he handled the first situation that confronted him.

The second problem which faced him, and which also caused a financial drain was that there were too many employees. Father Crowley settled it as follows. "It is not necessary to state that the help has been reduced fifty per cent. Against the sixty names on the payroll of last January, there are now thirty, with two boys, who receive a few dollars a month by way of encouragement for their services."

By July, 1893, Father Crowley had at St. Vincent's 431 boys between the ages of seven and fourteen. To assist him in the care of the boys, he had an assistant priest, Father Charles McMahon who had been appointed on April 17, 1893. Father McMahon devoted his time to the teaching of catechism and the discipline of the boys. "He intends to form sodalities in a short time and to organize societies for the smaller ones. He seems to have a special liking for the work."

The Dominican Sisters at that time numbered thirteen, still doing the domestic work and teaching all the grades in the school. Father Crowley also had definite ideas what a boy should eat; and he himself enumerated the menus, consisting of good bread, pretty good meat, good rice, good potatoes, excellent beans flavored with pork, pies, cake, soup, and milk. The abundance of coffee that the boys had had was eliminated by Father Crowley in favor of milk and chocolate. The shoe shop continued to operate, producing about twenty-five new pairs of shoes per week and repairing about twice that number.

It evidently was customary up to that time for the working-men to eat in the same dining room as the boys. Father Crowley felt that this was a cause of disturbance and therefore he immediately built a separate dining room which could accommodate thirty-five employees.

Next he turned his attention to the buildings themselves and to the grounds and farm. Fences were rebuilt, roads repaired, the play yards graveled, watered and rolled. Doors, locks, windows and stairways, all were given attention. On the farm, there were eighty-seven cows, and thirteen horses, eight of them very old. Father

Crowley traded four of the old ones for two fine young dray horses on the theory that "It is better to have a few good horses than a great many bad ones."

His main effort was centered upon the water problem. There had always been sufficient for the needs, but there was no surplus over and above the consumption, and in case of fire they were helpless. Father Crowley's first effort was to sink a new well, which seemed to have an abundance of water in it. But being a prudent man, he had it tested with a steam pump before erecting a windmill over it, and he found that the volume of water would not warrant such costly construction.

Then Father Crowley cast his eye across the road to the hills behind the Miller Ranch, on the property acquired by Father Croke some years previous. The land is described as follows:

> "Looking westward from the asylum the beautiful landscape is bounded by a beautiful range of hills which rise just back of Miller Hall, some five or six hundred feet above the tides. They are well covered with a varied forest growth, which suggested to the priests of those early days that these elevations had moisture, perhaps generous springs of water. On some warm summer days, when the luxuriant shade of the hill was inviting, the Fathers strolled up there and looked back at the Asylum, not forgetting to note that cool streams went singing down the canyons and found their way through shaded banks to the bay."

We have already noted that Father Croke installed the first pipe line from these hills to St. Vincent's. We also noted that Father McKinnon had men digging into the hill tunneling for water. Father Crowley pursued the same endeavor, still hoping to find somewhere in those hills a spring of such abundance that the water problem would be solved forever. In the fall of 1893, he set out into the hills in search. "At home in the saddle, and as easy and light on foot as the lithest lad in the home," he covered the hills very carefully. Often assisted by Father McMahon, he measured and dug and tried over again. Then he struck it. His efforts were so well rewarded that the Marin Journal which was never prone to use headlines came out on August 9, 1894 with the following:

"Marin JOURNAL, August 9, 1894.

New Water Works
BOUNTEOUS SUPPLY FOR ST. VINCENT'S

15,000 gallons Daily

Father Crowley's Efforts Crowned with Success
Consummation of a Splendid Enterprise for St. Vincent's Asylum

People who ride out Petaluma Avenue are often tempted by the hard and smooth road found after Puertosuello hill is crossed to go on past the Catholic Cemetery and Santa Margarita as far as the asylum. On the crown of the hill to the north of the avenue leading into the asylum a prominent object in the beautiful landscape is a new structure which at once attracts attention. It is graceful in its circular outline, but of such substantial appearance as to suggest that it is a fortification for defensive purposes, especially as the Stars and Stripes float in the breeze above it, and, you know, war was in the air but lately.

But it is not a fortification, for we rode into the asylum and asked Father Crowley. We perceived at once that it was a subject which interested him, and after a little conversation with him we did not wonder. The fort-like structure

IS A RESERVOIR

in which is stored a month's supply of mountain spring water, sufficient for all the necessities of the great institution, and thereby hangs a tale of no little interest. As soon as the supply of water had been discovered

THE RESERVOIR WAS BUILT

WHICH IS EXCAVATED IN SOLID GRANITE, AND LINED WITH CONCRETE, AND HAS AN ELEVATION OF 135 FEET ABOVE THE HIGHEST BUILDING. Then, with Father McMahon and about a dozen of his larger boys, he made his final survey, and strung about three miles of inch and a half pipe along the line. In a shady and sheltered canyon, 375 feet above the asylum, he built a storage reservoir, into which he led the main down the hillside, now in the ground, and again across the gulches on bridges, but always in the shade of the dense foliage, to the reservoir. Thence a two-inch pipe leads the water to the house, where it is directly connected with the plumbing. From the storage tanks in the hills to the Asylum is about 16,000 feet of pipe. The system has a capacity of 15,000 gallons a day, with a pressure that will throw a stream thirty feet above the highest building of the group. It has lessened the rate of insurance, which was very high, given the management a new feeling of security, a work that will make Father Crowley's administration famous in the annals of the asylum."

Father Crowley made another contribution to St. Vincent's of serious importance. On January 3, 1894, a meeting was held for the purpose of considering the incorporation of St. Vincent's.

The official corporation title, still in existence and still used in bequests and legacies is:

"St. Vincent's Roman Catholic Orphan
Asylum of San Francisco for Boys".

The first officers in the new corporation included Archbishop Riordan, President, by virtue of his office as Archbishop; and four priests: Fathers Patrick Scanlon, Thomas McSweeney, William B. O'Connor and Father Crowley. Four laymen: Frances D. Wensinger, John M. Burnett, James Coughlin and Andrew Carrigan were the other members of the Board of Directors.

Father Crowley's water contribution to St. Vincent's came at the very end of his administration. Already in March, 1894 it was known that the Brothers were preparing to take over St. Vincent's. On June 12, 1894, Archbishop Riordan wrote to the Mother General of the Dominican Sisters as follows: "I cannot say just now on what precise day the Brothers will go to the Asylum. I will arrange matters so as to put the Sisters to as little inconvenience as possible."

On August 2, 1894 an article appeared in the Marin *Journal* which gave the matter an air of finality.

"Rev. Father Crowley will retire soon from the management of the St. Vincent's Orphan Asylum for Boys. The change will take place about the middle of this month when the Christian Brotherhood will assume charge. Father Crowley will return to the Superintendency of the Youths Directory in San Francisco which he left to come here, and which is intimately connected with the Asylum since it is there that all the boys are received who enter the Asylum. He was therefore no stranger to this institution when he took charge, and in leaving, he by no means severs all official relations with it."

The date of the change-over was finally set for August 15, 1894. On that day the priests of the Archdiocese ceased to be the Directors of St. Vincent's and the Dominican Sisters retired from their labors after twenty-six years. Not even their names have been preserved—except by the Recording Angel. Their going away is tersely recorded even in their own archives: "August 15, 1894. The Sisters came home from the Orphan Asylum".

Father Crowley[13] stayed for a few weeks to acquaint the Brothers with the running of the institution and to serve as their chaplain until the Archbishop would appoint a new one. St. Vincent's was ready to begin a new life.

CHAPTER XIII

LIFE BEGINS AT FORTY
1895 - 1905

With the arrival of the Christian Brothers on August 15, 1894, St. Vincent's was well into its fortieth year. Life for the next twenty-eight years was to be different from anything previous. It was strictly a man's institution now. Men taught in the school, men prefected the dormitories, the play yards, the dining room. Men were exclusively in charge of every department.

Appointed to supervise this entire enterprise was Brother Michael. Like so many of his priest-predecessors in the office of Director, Brother had been born in Ireland, in Glen-Carrignavar, County Cork in 1855. He was the son of Cornelius and Mary Dorgan. He had entered the novitiate of the Christian Brothers at Martinez, California on July 19, 1880 and made his first vows as a religious on June 16, 1882. His first teaching assignment was at Sacred Heart College in San Francisco. On January 28, 1886 he was transferred to St. Michael's College in Portland, Oregon where he taught for two years. On July 16, 1888 he was appointed Director of that school. Some time shortly before his assignment to St. Vincent's, Brother Michael was made Director of St. Mary's College in Oakland. On June 26, 1894 he received his appointment as Director of St. Vincent's.

Besides carefully selecting the new Director of St. Vincent's, the higher superiors of the Christian Brothers had made other careful plans in preparing to take over the Orphanage. Three Brothers who had the necessary experience had been sent out from New York. They were Brothers Candidus, Abrasian, and Azary. The remaining Brothers who arrived at St. Vincent's on August 15, 1894 were Brothers Leo, James, Fidelis, Basil, Austin, Lactain, Valdibertus and Vandiliman. These made up the first faculty and instituted the methods that were common to all Christian Brothers' Institutions.

There was no great reorganization; simply different emphasis placed on various parts of the daily routine. The religious program received a new impetus. Always devoted advocates of the Baltimore Catechism, the Brothers made the religious instruction the core of their daily program. The day commenced with Mass and the class in religion was first and foremost. Careful preparation was made for First Communion and Confirmation. We find the first mention of the Forty Hours Devotion at St. Vincent's, for that religious function was held commencing December 23 until Christmas Day, 1894.

The recreational life was also attended to by the Brothers, and we find the first mention of football and baseball in an article in the Monitor of December 22, 1894. Shortly after things were settled, Brother Michael resurrected the Band which had come and gone so many times during the past twenty years. The Band of thirty-four pieces, now organized under Brother Fidelis, was to persevere for many years and in its own way would bring many fine benefits to the boys who participated.

The Faculty in 1909—Standing: Brother Fabian, Brother Frederick, Brother Nicholas, Brother Albian, Brother Patrick. Sitting: Brother Jerome, Brother Dionysius, Brother Xenophon, Brother Adrian, Brother James.

The Band with Brother Xenophon and Mr. Schultz, the bandmaster.

A group of boys with Brother Xenophon and Brother Dionysius.

The number of boys who were present when the Brothers took over was about 425. Although Father Crowley had reduced the population and more carefully selected the applicants than his predecessors, the number rapidly rose again under the Brothers. During July, August and September, 1894, forty new boys entered St. Vincent's. The list of names and ages published in the Marin Journal in November shows the drop off in preponderance of Irish names and also shows that the boys entering in 1894 were, for the most part, older than the entrants of ten years previous. Most of the forty were around eleven years of age.

The Marin Journal is very silent concerning St. Vincent's during these years. Our first glimpse inside the school during Brother Michael's years is found in the Monitor on July 20, 1895:

> "*About a year ago, the Christian Brothers took charge of St. Vincent's Orphan Asylum near San Rafael. They have inaugurated manual training and have succeeded very well in this project. There is a large area of uncultivated land surrounding the Asylum, which the Brothers desire to use for an orchard. During Father Crowley's management of the institution a quantity of marsh land was reclaimed. Brother Azary a noted botanist and horticulturist, is to make experiments with the soil with a view of placing as much as possible in the orchard. His examination will be very thorough, and on the results of his tests will depend the kind of trees to be planted. Brother Azary joined the order of Christian Brothers nearly forty years ago, and has made a specialty of horticulture. In France he was attached for a number of years to the Agricultural College conducted by the Brothers on the Bouree about seventy miles from Paris. He has also been connected with all the other agricultural colleges of the Brothers throughout the world, and has been spending some time on this coast. His principal labors in this country have been in New York and the southern States.*"

Thus we see the first mention of the trade school inaugurated by the Brothers. This included the expansion of the work done in the shoe shop, and a new enterprise, a tailor shop for the purpose of making the clothing worn by the boys. This trade school differed from the one started by Father McKinnon in that the Brothers adhered strictly to the "under fourteen years of age" policy. Thus the boys taught in these shops by the Brothers were younger than the ones cared for in Father McKinnon's trade school.

It is obvious from this that the Brothers were economical. Boys over fourteen were "farmed out" because there was no income to support them. The Brothers seem to have felt that the enormous debt of ninety-five thousand dollars devolved upon them, although it really was not their responsibility. A couple of legacies received at this time helped to reduce this indebtedness. The first was the will of Joseph Donohue of San Francisco who had for many years been a friend of St. Vincent's. He left the sum of $5,000 in April, 1895. The second was the long contested will of James Mervyn Donahue of the railroad family which was finally settled in 1896. The Marin *Journal* of August 6, 1896 carried the following notice:

> "*In the matter of the estate of J. M. Donahue, the final account has been settled and the estate distributed. The charitable bequests were found to aggregate more than one third of the estate which could be legally donated to charity, so all the bequests were scaled to give each its proportion of funds available. St. Vincent's Orphan Asylum legacy of $20,000 is therefore reduced to $13,350 and all others in proportion.*"

On October 17, 1896 another article in the Monitor described what was going on in St. Vincent's:

> "*St. Vincent's Orphan Asylum, San Rafael, has presented a lively scene for the past three weeks. A large force of men has been employed daily in putting down bituminous rock in a vast playground for the boys. When completed, the playground will be the largest and best of its kind in the State. In winter the children will be protected from mud and in the summer from dust. Carpenters are busily engaged in arranging the gymnasium and other places of recreation for the amusement of the orphans, and there seems to be nothing left undone to promote the spiritual, intellectual and physical welfare of the little ones.*
> *To the eye of the observant, a great change has been wrought in the surroundings of the Asylum. The orchards under the hand of cultivation have improved beyond expectation, while the garden abounds with choice vegetables in sufficient quantities to supply the wants of the six hundred inmates of the institution.*"

With this article we see that the population of St. Vincent's is again at capacity. This explains the very large Confirmation classes of June 25, 1896 and September 28, 1898. There were about 160 boys each time. These Confirmation classes were instructed by the Brothers and examined by the Chaplain, Father Joseph Phelan. With the appointment of Father Phelan as Chaplain on September 13, 1894, there came to St. Vincent's a priest whose life story is very colorful. Whereas under Father McKinnon, the school had been the scene of a horse raising enterprise, it was now to be the locale for poetic composition.

Classroom scene in 1909—Some of the names on the blackboard are: Martin Quinn, Ernest Clark, Vincent Guerin, Peter Riley, John Kingbery.

The Tailor Shop in 1909.

Joseph Phelan was born in Rathdowney, Queens County, Ireland on September 8, 1839. He came to the United States on September 19, 1857 and arrived in San Francisco on November 4, 1857. This eighteen year old youth headed for the mines and spent the next nine years working in Nevada County, mostly at Cherokee and at Grass Valley. Then came the vocation to the priesthood such as we have already witnessed in the case of Father McKinnon. Joseph Phelan was twenty-seven years old when he commenced his studies, spending one year, 1866-1867 at St. Mary's College in Oakland. The following year he returned to Ireland and for three years studied at Mt. Mellary Seminary. His four years of theology were taken at All Hallows Seminary in Dublin. He was ordained a priest on June 24, 1874. He immediately returned to the scene of his labors and for two years was the assistant priest in Grass Valley, the parish that cared for Cherokee.

Father Phelan describes himself at this time in the following words: "Not being a man of much ability, and having no early training, being old and having a bad voice, I merely struggled through college. But being ordained, everything changed. I was a different man; everything prospered with me." On September 19, 1876 Father Phelan was moved to Austin, Nevada, where he remained as Pastor for eighteen years. A contemporary describes Father Phelan during this period:

> "He is not remarkable for his brilliant oratorical powers, but he is distinguished by far more valuable qualifications. He is a pious, zealous, amiable young priest, of the most solid moral principles, and might not be inaptly termed a second 'Cure of Ars' in Nevada. He aims at nothing extraordinary, but by his mild, gentle and unassuming demeanor, does more, and is calculated to do more for religion, than if his eloquence rivaled that of Demosthenes."

This was the priest who, to the sorrow of Austin, Nevada, was appointed to be Chaplain at St. Vincent's on September 4, 1894. He arrived there on September 14, 1894 and for the next nine years worked together with the Brothers for the spiritual welfare of the boys. During these years, Father Phelan, now fifty-five years old, had a great deal of leisure time. He was only the Chaplain, not the Administrator as had been his priest predecessors. He used his leisure time to finish a book of poetry that he had commenced in Austin. The book, now out of print, contains a poem for St. Patrick's Day written for St. Vincent's boys on February 27, 1895. Another one, written on August 21, 1896 is called "Joe Neppert", evidently one of the boys. His longest work entitled "My Jubilee", was written in commemoration of the twenty-fifth anniversary of his ordination which he celebrated on June 24, 1899. Father Phelan evidently missed the missionary life, for he wrote of himself: "I was better adapted for a missionary priest than scribbling poetry to fill up leisure time." There was a good deal of truth in this, for Father Phelan's poetry was rather versification than true poetry. But, no matter what may be said regarding the poetic quality of his writings, the reader cannot but be impressed by the deeply religious spirit that permeates the whole book. Father Phelan had his book published in San Francisco in 1902. He entitled it: "Poetical Works and Biographical Remarks of Rev. Joseph Phelan."

The following year, on February 15, 1903, Father Phelan died at St. Mary's Hospital on Rincon Hill in San Francisco. His funeral took place from Sacred Heart Church. Father Cassin, a former assistant at St. Vincent's preached the eulogy in which he referred to the genial, self-sacrificing nature of Father Phelan. The boys at St. Vincent's must certainly have missed this kind and charitable priest.

Father Phelan's loss to St. Vincent's was followed within two years by the loss of Brother Michael[14]. On August 31, 1905, the Marin *Journal* carried the following notice:

> "Brother Michael, the popular and efficient superintendent of St. Vincent's Orphan Asylum is ill at St. Joseph's Hospital. He will have to undergo a serious operation. During his illness Brother Xenophon has charge."

Thus St. Vincent's was ready for a new Director just as it entered its golden jubilee years.

CHAPTER XIV

GOLDEN JUBILEE YEARS
1905 - 1918

The illness of Brother Michael proved to be serious enough for his superiors to realize that he would not be able to work for a long time and that a new Director should be appointed for St. Vincent's. Accordingly on August 18, 1905, Brother Xenophon was transferred from Sacred Heart College, where he had been the Director, to St. Vincent's. Brother Michael's illness lasted over three months, and it was not until January, 1906 that he received a new assignment, that of Director of St. Joseph's Academy in Berkeley.

The new Director of St. Vincent's, Brother Xenophon Cyril, (1812-1929) was a veteran of many years experience. He was forty-three years old at the time of his appointment and had been a Christian Brother twenty years. Born William Kelly in Santa Rosa on September 24, 1862, the son of Daniel and Julia Kelly he had entered the Christian Brothers on August 18, 1876. From them he received his education and training as a teacher and made his first vows as a religious on June 17, 1885. His assignments were many. In the course of his many years of teaching he taught practically every grade, but the fifth fell to his lot three different times. On his various assignments he had acted as Infirmarian and Prefect of Clothing. Having been stationed in Oakland, San Francisco, Sacramento and Martinez, he was aware of those parts of the Bay area from which St. Vincent's boys were received. This man of experience now took over the administration of St. Vincent's.

He had fifteen Brothers to assist him in the care of about 500 boys. The school day ran from nine o'clock until twelve o'clock and from one-thirty until four o'clock. Because Saturday was a busy day, a day of work at household chores, Brother Xenophon instituted a half holiday on Wednesday afternoons to make up to the boys the time devoted to cleaning and scrubbing.

A reporter from the San Francisco *Call* in 1909 described the various amusements of the boys during playtime. Flying of kites, skating in the paved play yard, dancing of various step dances, and rope jumping were named. In fact, the reporter visited the hero of the rope jumpers in the Infirmary, a little fellow whose legs were swollen because he had broken the record with 4,500 jumps.

The same writer tells the problem facing the Brothers when a boy became fourteen years of age. Instead of being able to keep the boy and further his education, he had to be sent away since the State cut off all aid at that age. The policy employed is described as follows:

> *"When the boys reach fourteen years of age, Brother Xenophon tries first of all to place them in the country. Applications for them are investigated by the priests of the parishes from which they come. The child then placed out is watched over, if possible by the neighboring priest. Other than this, the aid of the Children's Agency of the Associated Charities is solicited in investigation and follow-up.*
>
> *In the matter of placing children out, this institution is handicapped, as every other one is, by the fact that comparatively few children are eligible for home placing and adoption. The are too many unworthy "surviving parents", or other negligent relatives who do nothing for the child's support, but come forward when the child is fourteen and has an earning capacity. They do not supplement the work of the state in trying to rear the children who have been deprived of a parent. They shift all the responsibility and come forward proudly with an air of proprietorship when the child is, or can easily be made self-supporting. A recent case in point involved a boy who had been most advantageously placed in a family. A mother, who by her neglect, had no moral right to jurisdiction over the boy, demanded and had to be given · his whereabouts. The boy was taken from his home, and now those who know the circumstances are praying that all will be well with the lad, who has lost a splendid opportunity."*

The *Call* proceeds to tell Brother Xenophon's hopes and plans.

> *"Brother Xenophon is trusting that the new law for the establishment of a trade school for orphans and half orphans will round out his endeavor. He would keep his boys after fourteen or until they are proficient enough to be self-supporting. He would have money enough to individualize his boys by the cottage system, or at least some phases of it. But until that time comes, he lays all possible emphasis on the best that is available. He finds music one of the most grateful channels along which to carry his boys. He has the best possible leader for the band, the work of which is far more polished than that of many professional bands."*

Needless to say, the dream of Brother Xenophon[15] was not realized. After five years as Director of St. Vincent's, he was chosen to the highest office in the San Francisco District and was made the Brother Visitor on February 17, 1910.

Immediately there was need of a new Director, and Brother Xenophon, who now had the selecting to do, chose Brother Paul (1870-1913), the Director of Holy Cross School in Santa Cruz. Francis J. Martin, as he was born, was the son of Thomas and Mary Martin. He had been born in Marysville, California on October 3, 1870. He entered the Christian Brothers at Martinez on March 13, 1886, and made his first vows on June 26, 1889. He had been stationed in Oakland three separate times, and once in Sacramento, San Francisco, and Santa Cruz. His administration of St. Vincent's was to endure for five years during which two major events took place at St. Vincent's.

The first of these was announced in the *Monitor* on September 2, 1911.

> "A new dormitory and refectory costing $92,955 will soon be under construction as an addition to St. Vincent's Orphan Asylum. The contract specifies that the building shall be two stories and a half high, of brick, steel and reinforced concrete and shall be completed within six months. The structure will be lighted with electricity."

This new building was the fruition of plans made by the Board of Directors at their meeting on March 8, 1906. Their decision to rebuild St. Vincent's was now beginning to be realized. The financing of such a program was a large undertaking but it was realized by the Archbishop by means of a collection. On August 3, 1912 he announced an assessment on each parish in the Archdiocese to help pay for the construction work at St. Vincent's. For the next few months the *Monitor* records many events sponsored by the various parishes as means of meeting their assessments. Many of them exceeded their goal, so generous was the response of the people to the appeal. On April 17, 1913 the completed assessment was published, showing that the parishes had oversubscribed. The total collected was $102,008.00

The new building was definitely worthy of the hopes of the Archbishop and his devoted people. It was a long structure joined to one end of Father McKinnon's wing of 1889. It extended out to the south, at a right angle to the main south wing of St. Vincent's.

The lower floor contained three large dining rooms for the boys, with terraza floors, and windows on both sides. A very large well equipped kitchen extending the full width of the building was next. Then followed a large refrigerator with separate divisions for meat, dairy products and vegetables. Next to it were store rooms, dining rooms for the employees and a new bake shop. On the floor above, were three dormitories, each one capable of holding 125 beds. Solid brick walls separated each dormitory and a steel fire door closed the opening between them. Two large washrooms were located on the same floor, one at each end. In each of these was a long porcelain wash trough with sufficient faucets to provide water for each boy. Long lockers for clothes and small closed boxes for brushes, combs, tooth brushes etc., lined the sides and ends of the washrooms. A small room off each dormitory was provided for the attending Brother. Outside fire escapes along one side led to the ground floor as an added fire protection. A large airy clothes room was located at the south end directly above the bake shop.

Into this new building in 1912, Brother Paul moved the small and middle-sized boys. The older ones still occupied one of the older buildings.

The second event which occurred during the time of Brother Paul's administration was the establishment of the Christian Brothers Training School on the grounds of St. Vincent's

In a general meeting of the Brother Visitors of the United States held in New York in October, 1912, it was decided to open a central Scholasticate for the whole United States, with the exception of the San Francisco District, which, because of its isolation, should open its own. It was to be a kind of normal school, a teacher training institute to prepare the newly professed novices for their life work. The rule of the Christian Brothers required at least one year of such preparation. Permission was obtained from the Archbishop for the Training School to be established at St. Vincent's. In order to prepare for it, the Brothers had sent one of their number, Brother Joseph to visit the normal schools of Europe in special preparation for this work.

Brother Joseph arrived home on August 13, 1913. He found that preparation had been underway at St. Vincent's for the establishment of the School. Brother Xenophon, the Visitor, and Brother Paul had set aside one wing in the front on the north side as the home of the New Training School. It consisted of a very fine chapel, a classroom, a room for demonstration lessons, a fully equipped recreation room, and a dormitory with twelve beds. Brother Joseph found the place already furnished.

On August 21, 1913, accompanied by the Master of Novices, Brother Victorinus Leo, seven Student Brothers arrived from the Novitiate at Martinez. On the following day classes commenced in the new school. It was officially named the "Training School". The Student Brothers were in no way connected with the St. Vincent's Community. Their quarters were separate, they had their own chapel, their own classes and their own Director, Brother Joseph. They remained in the front garden for their walks. Their free time during the first year was spent in painting and renovating their new home. In class they studied the subjects they were going to teach; they also had special classes in pedagogy, and three days a week they did practice teaching in the school at St. Vincent's. This was where the Orphanage benefited, because the very presence of these Student Brothers in the classroom insured the best possible demonstration teaching on the part of the faculty of St. Vincent's. Besides, Brother Joseph was officially the Inspector for St. Vincent's school, and his presence also insured the best possible teaching. Unfortunately Brother Joseph was not able to inspect as much as he wished. He himself had classes to prepare in order to teach the Student Brothers and he had only one Brother to assist him. Brother Cornelius came over from St. Mary's College every Wednesday afternoon to give a course in drawing. From time to time other teachers came in to help instruct the Brothers in the Scholasticate.

Three more novices arrived in January, 1914, but their presence presented a problem because they were four months behind the original seven in their studies and there were not enough instructors to commence a new course for these three. Therefore they were given grades to teach in the school at St. Vincent's and supervised as they taught. Although the three did well enough, the Brothers decided to accept Student Brothers only once a year.

The presence of the Training School brought about a couple of minor historical events. The Spring Convention of the Christian Brothers of the Pacific Coast was held at St. Vincent's in March, 1914, and one of the Student Brothers taught a catechism lesson, an effort which pleased the visitors and awakened wholesome discussion. The Stations of the Cross were canonically erected in the chapel of the Training School on March 27, 1914. The first fifteen day retreat ever held in the District began at the Training School on Sunday, July 19, 1914, with Father Giacobbi, S.J., as the Spiritual Director. The retreat was made by the ten Student Brothers, by the seven new ones scheduled to begin their courses and by several Brothers from other houses. At the end of the retreat, the little chapel was the scene of profession of first vows by two of the novices.

On August 17, 1914 the second year of the Training School was opened with the seven new scholastics as students. These completed their course on June 24, 1915. They went for retreat to St. Joseph's in Berkeley. Three weeks later they received their assignments. Two were sent home as lacking true vocations. Brothers Victor and Dominic were given classes at St. Vincent's. Brother Matthias was retained as an Instructor in the Training School. Brother Coleman was appointed to Berkeley and Brother Adolphus was sent to Sacred Heart in San Francisco. So far the Training School was proving very satisfactory.

It was at this point that another major change came in the administration of St. Vincent's. Brother Paul[16] was sent back as Director of Holy Cross school in Santa Cruz, and St. Vincent's received a new Director in the person of Brother Florinus Peter (1875-1933). He was older than any previous Director upon assuming his new position. Having been born Richard James Doyle at Arthur, Ontario, Canada on February 19, 1857, he was fifty-eight years old at this time. He had entered the Christian Brothers, first at St. Louis, and then transferred to the Novitiate at Oakland where he made his vows on July 1, 1878. He had held nineteen different assignments before coming to St. Vincent's. He had been at St. Mary's College four different times, the last time in 1910 as Director. His labors had taken him to Christian Brothers' schools in Vancouver, Washington and Sacramento, California. Five times he had been at St. Joseph's in Oakland, the last time as Director. He came from that position to St. Vincent's. During the years of his administration life continued rather routinely at St. Vincent's.

The Training School commenced its third year with eight new Student Brothers and the two from the previous year who were teaching in the school at St. Vincent's. This year, 1916, marked another first in the life of St. Vincent's. On the first Friday of January, Exposition of the Blessed Sacrament was held in the chapel of the Training School for the first time.

The Training School opened in 1917 with six new Student Brothers. This group had an experience not shared by previous Scholastics. They taught in a Vacation School held for the boys at St. Vincent's. Besides the teachers being themselves new, the boys did not care for the idea of school during vacation. The experiment was tried again the following year and then dropped.

This year, 1917, St. Vincent's had less boys than for many previous years. The enrollment had dropped to 286 boys, as compared with 400 in 1913 and about the same number in 1915. Of the 286 St. Vincent's was given aid directly by the State for 134. The rest presented a new arrangement. They were wards of thirteen Juvenile Courts, not for delinquency but for support. These Courts were in turn reimbursed by the State. We see here the beginning of the Counties assuming responsibility for the children from their areas. Perhaps it was the drop in the enrollment that had induced the Brothers to begin at this time to accept from the Juvenile Courts problem boys as a matter of policy.

Brother Peter, being a practical man, made several improvements at St. Vincent's. He discarded the long tables in the dining room and substituted small ones seating four boys each. He also introduced table cloths in order to give a more home-like atmosphere to the dining room. At this time the menu seemed somewhat more generous than anything seen previously. On one occasion the boys had bread, rice and milk with coffee for breakfast. Soup, spaghetti, beef steak with gravy, potatoes and bread made up the noon meal; while fried potatoes, stewed fruit and bread with milk constituted the supper.

A visitor to St. Vincent's in January, 1917 wrote the following report concerning the school:

> "The system of school is good. I heard the boys read and spell and found them well trained. The Supervisor of Instruction, Brother Joseph, is a very progressive teacher and keeps in touch with modern methods of

*education. He informed me that a recent examination of the school
resulted in a recommendation in all subjects except arithmetic which
he is now planning to bring up to standard. The books in use are the
State series and a history of the Holy Bible. There are nine teachers
and six student coaches who are assisting the backward boys. This is an
excellent plan. No class has more than forty pupils."*

The Training School when it reopened for its fifth year on
August 15, 1917 had eight Student Brothers, one of them Brother
Comgall James coming from the Scholasticate in Casletown, Ireland.

One realizes, of course, from the date that the United States
was now involved in World War I. This would actually work a
severe hardship on Brother Peter's administration; but to his credit,
he was able to manage very successfully as can be seen from the following financial report for 1917 which has been preserved:

ORDINARY RECEIPTS		*ORDINARY MAINTENANCE EXPENSES*	
Counties	$17,863.52	*Pay roll*	$13,856.96
Boarders	7,556.20	*Repairs to bldgs.*	932.47
State	8,545.77	*Miscellaneous*	6,536.13
		Taxes	1,178.06
		Fuel and light	8,763.17
		School	282.69
		Bedding	81.20
		BALANCE	7,334.81
Totals	$33,965.49		$33,965.49

The BALANCE gave an allowance of $2.26 per month for
food, clothing, etc., for each boy on the basis of 270 boys, the
average number of boys in the institution for the year 1917. The
remaining $25,284.32 that it cost to run the institution was made
up from the farm supplies, bequests and donations, and by the
Archbishop. Under the heading Miscellaneous were included the
following items: postage, printing, stationery, express, freight, laundry and dairy supplies, pumps and laundry machinery, repairs to
ranges, belts, hose, machine oil, kitchen utensils, fruit cans, installation of pasteurizing plant and auto repairs.

On July 28, 1918 Brother Peter[17] was relieved of his responsibility and was sent to St. Mary's College to be bookkeeper. His
successor, the last Christian Brother Director took over on the
same day. Trying times were ahead as St. Vincent's entered its
sixty-third year of life.

CHAPTER XV

OLD AGE AND INFIRMITIES
1918 - 1921

Brother Vellesian (1870-1950), as the new Director was called in religion, had been born Henry Mallon in Portland, Oregon on July 17, 1870. He was the first candidate from St. Michael's College in Portland to enter the Christian Brothers. On May 1, 1886, he began his religious life in the Novitiate at Martinez, California. His first vows were made on July 22, 1888. His assignments were mostly at St. Mary's College where he eventually became the Director on June 19, 1904, for six years and then again on August 1, 1914. Previous to his coming to St. Vincent's he had been commissioned by the Brothers to recruit candidates for the novitiate. Therefore, when he arrived to take over as Director of St. Vincent's, he already knew the new group of four Student Brothers who were to start their year in the Training School on August 17, 1918.

Vocations to the Brotherhood had already been affected by the war; now the Training School felt its effect. In the new class, one of the four was not capable of the studies; another had to be sent to fill in a vacancy in Santa Cruz. This left only two Studdent Brothers. On February 18, 1918 these two, Brother Augustine and Brother Bernard were given classes to teach at St. Vincent's. Therefore the Training School was forced to close its doors, never to reopen at St. Vincent's. Brother Joseph was given the duty of recruiting vocations which Brother Vellesian had just left. The Training School, brought to a sudden and unexpected end after six years, had served the Asylum well. St. Vincent's had been the scene of training for thirty-seven Student Brothers.

Brother Vellesian's first year at St. Vincent's, 1918, is described in very great detail in a report sent to the Archbishop by Doctor Mary Harriss, an agent of the State Board of Control who resided at St. Vincent's from July 11 to July 20, 1918, during a regular inspection tour by the State. She gives in her report, her appreciation, criticisms and recommendations. She also tells us what life was like in 1918.

Although the institution had a capacity for 525 children there were only 265 there in July, 1918, a few being away on vacation. The children were divided according to the following age groups.

6 - 8	9 - 10	12 - 13	14 - 16	over 16
32	96	108	42	8

The sources from which these children came were listed by Dr. Harriss as follows:

"Children are obtained from the Juvenile Court and from parents or guardians who commit their children to the Brothers' care. Of these, at present, there are 15 whole orphans, 64 half orphans, 120 court children, 4 abandoned children and 62 so-called boarders. The Juvenile Court is represented by the following counties:

San Francisco...67	Marin 4	San Joaquin.... 3
Fresno 3	Nevada 1	Alameda 7
Merced 6	Sacramento 5	Santa Barbara.. 1
Santa Clara 2	Yolo 1	Catholic Humane
San Mateo 8	Contra Costa..... 3	Bureau 15

The average cost per month for each boy for the six months ending June 30, 1918 was $16.80."

This report shows a tremendous difference both in number and in classification of the boys of St. Vincent's since 1888. The number of orphans and half orphans had certainly diminished. The terms "orphanage" and "Orphan Asylum" were becoming misnomers.

The Daily Program for the boys was as follows:

6:45	Rise
7:15	Mass
8:00	Breakfast, followed by chores and play
10:00 to 12:45	School
1:00	Dinner
2:00 to 4:30	School, followed by band, chores and play
7:00	Supper, followed by play and study
9:00	Washroom
9:30	Bed in summer.

Concerning the Brothers and their school program, the Report states as follows:

> "The staff of Brothers has been well trained for teaching and other branches in the various schools of their Order or other Colleges and have a national reputation as trainers of youth. They are on constant duty with these boys and have only short vacations. The teachers are drawn from the ranks of the Christian Brothers and the young scholastics in training for their Community, many of whom are graduates of Colleges or schools of the Order or from public schools. Many are men of superior attainments.
>
> The class rooms are in the oldest part of the building, and may have been built for that purpose, but have changed about from time to time, partitions taken down and erected, and are neither very clean nor well lighted, with not very great blackboard space, old fashioned desks and seats, many of which seat two boys. There are eight grades as in the public schools and about 35 or 40 pupils in each class. There is no kindergarten and no special class or training for retarded or defective children. Some of the children seem to have exceptional talent in drawing and some clever cartoonists have done their initial work in this school."

The description of the boys' clothing together with the pictures of these boys in the early 1900's are almost humorous.

> "Clothing is adapted to the needs and habits of rough boys, is muchly mended for day and yard wear, but neat and clean on Sundays and during the school sessions. Overalls are in general use with short khaki coats and a very superfluous string of a necktie is insisted upon even in hot summer weather, possessing neither utility nor aesthetic value. Shoes are shabby around the yards and farm. The rocky and sandy soil being hard on them. A shoemaker and numerous boy helpers are kept constantly employed mending. Sundays and holidays the boys are well shod and very tidy. A good outfit of clothing is given each orphan upon his leaving the Institution."

The Report then proceeds to state that the older boys considered it a privilege to get out into the fields for farm work, dairying, fruit picking, tending the chickens, hogs and dogs. "Indeed, they, under the direction of some of the Brothers do nearly all the work of the farm."

In regard to Father Thomas McKeon, the Chaplain at that time, Dr. Harriss stated: "A very kind, but firm young chaplain, who has been two years in the Institution, seems to have a very wholesome influence in bringing the boys to a proper sense of their moral obligation to one another and the community, and his kindness to them and trust reposed in them seems to meet a hearty response, which makes him very much beloved."

For the first time in our story we get a description of the leisure time activities and opportunities.

"The boys have a movie show every week sent by some film corporation from San Rafael. There are occasional lectures and theatricals in which the boys themselves take part, quite nice programs being presented. Hand ball, basketball and baseball are all favorite sports indulged in on their large playground and led by one of the professors. On his birthday each child may present himself at the office and the Secretary gives him a prize package and a bag of candy. There seems to be no boys' library on the place, a sad reflection on the institution. Occasional magazines and other periodicals which come their way, including the funny page of the local papers, are passed from hand to hand and devoured by many of the boys. Others again have no taste for reading, nor does there seem much inducement in what is offered them in an endeavor to cultivate such taste. Of course, some reading must be correlated with their school work, but on the whole most of it comprised within the contents of the State readers.

The nice matron in her sewing room has a few toys and small games and the middle sized boys consider it a great privilege to go there, help in the darning and play with the contents of "mother's" game locker. Some of them will spend hours with a mechanical or constructive game. Most of such toys are donated, Christmas being harvest season for them. Again there is need for organized play and a good leader to teach these children real boys' games and various kinds of handcraft. A few rings and bars in the yard are the only attempts at gymnasium. There should be swings, seesaws, ladders, horizontal and parallel bars with a qualified playground director who could give his attention also to club, dumb-bell and other corrective gymnastic exercises. One of the lay professors with a keen interest in baseball trains a good team in that sport and they tell with justifiable pride of the games they have won, showing what a factor in their scholastic training wholesome sport might be made."

In regard to the work done by the boys, which has always been part of their training, the Report states that there was no formal vocational training, but what was given was utilitarian for the good of the house. Opportunities for work in the house, laundry, kitchen, garden, farm, bake shop, cobbling and tailor shops and dairy were afforded before and after school hours and in the vacation period.

The Band received special notice in the following statements: "The musical education of St. Vincent's boys is quite superior. They devote a great deal of time to practice for their brass band, which is a well known feature of the Institution. Their good knowledge of music has furnished many of them a splendid means of livelihood upon leaving their Alma Mater."

The final point which the Report discusses and takes to task is the Infirmary set-up. As was usual with all inspectors and visitors, the good health of the boys was noted. But Dr. Harriss, fresh with the new experiences gained in the war brings to the attention of the Brothers and the Archbishop a new note, that of preventive medicine. The Infirmary in 1918 had two locations, one in one of the old buildings where there were eighteen beds in two large rooms; then there was the isolation cottage with ten beds, large porches and a separate play area for the convalescents. This entire Infirmary set-up had been cared for by a faithful employee, Mr. John Clifford, for twenty years. Although Mr. Clifford's experience included Bellevue and Lane Hospitals, the Doctor states that he was not up to date. "St. Vincent's has been especially fortunate in having few epidemics, but such exemption should not make the Directors overconfident." There follows then a full page of recommendations for bringing the Infirmary procedure up to the latest standards. One recommendation was that the school employ a competent resident trained nurse who could do a great deal of the preventive work outlined.

Such was life at St. Vincent's in Brother Vellesian's days. The enrollment in 1919 was 356 boys and in 1920 there were 334 children. The staff consisted of fourteen Brothers, and three lay people. Brother Vellesian tried constantly to keep ahead of the deterioration of the buildings. The building erected by Sister Frances was now sixty-five years old, and Father Lootens' was fifty-six. Even the newest of the ones erected by Father Croke was forty years old. Brother Vellesian was constantly hampered by insufficient funds, trying, as all the Brother Directors did, to keep within the budget of their income. In 1919 he hired a woman housekeeper to look after the dormitories. In January, 1920, he found the desired trained nurse, Miss M. O'Sullivan, who did a great deal for the health of the boys while she was at St. Vincent's. Negotiations for more new buildings were pending, but the war stopped everything temporarily. A visiting nurse in 1920 writes on behalf of the Brothers: "It would be most unjust to blame the Order of Christian Brothers for the conditions as these men are crippled both financially and by lack of assistants."

After the Christmas donations of 1920, Brother Vellesian ordered new playground equipment for the play yard. He also arranged to have the Administration building repainted. In every possible way he tried to keep abreast of the times and follow the recommendations made. But he was definitely hampered by lack of staff and lack of money. It was obvious that some vast change would be necessary. For one thing, new buildings were absolutely necessary.

The change came indeed, but of a most unexpected nature. On August 2, 1921, Archbishop Hanna[18] received the following letter from Brother Joseph, who was at that time the Brother Visitor of the District.

> *"Most Reverend and dear Archbishop:*
> *Following our conversations and conferences of several months relative to St. Vincent's, we called a special meeting of our Advisory Council and found not a dissenting voice from the plan as originally suggested to your Grace.*
> *Hence we most respectfully make formal application, on behalf of our Superior General, for permission to withdraw our Brothers from St. Vincent's at your convenience."*

The letter then continues with a very clear explanation of the reason why the Brothers were forced into this decision.

> *"No one understands more clearly than Your Grace the status of the educational conditions into which we are so suddenly come. Before the war, thirty to forty boys made up our normal first year high school class, a sufficiency for a teacher, surely. Today in one of our schools, we have registered well nigh two hundred applicants for this same class. Others of our institutions are almost similarly situated. All of which means that from three to five Brothers are now needed to teach in the lower high school classes to do the task of one of past years, while a relatively like condition must arise in the upper classes as promotions are successively made. Hence our desire to transfer the personnel of St. Vincent's to other of our schools as a measure of immediate relief to overworked Brothers and congested classes, believing that Sisters will prove equal to the needs of St. Vincent's."*

This was certainly a change, but a most surprising one. It was not unexpected, however, by the Archbishop. Evidently Brother Joseph had previously informed him of the plans contemplated. Meanwhile the Archbishop had been busy seeing what could be done if and when the Brothers did withdraw. He was ready, therefore, when he got Brother Joseph's letter, to reply as follows on

August 10, 1921: "After consultation with the Sisters of St. Dominic at Mission San Jose, I am able to inform you that they will take over the most of the Asylum at San Rafael in August, 1922. I can only tell you how much I regret that your great need of teachers compels you to leave the work to which you have consecrated such fine ability."

The problem now before the Archbishop was to obtain teachers, because the Dominican Sisters had agreed to take over only the domestic work at St. Vincent's, similar to the work of their predecessors, the Dominican Sisters of San Rafael in the days of Father Birmingham and Father Croke. A solution was reached indeed, but one which is most unique in the history of California. Its very existence was to bring St. Vincent's almost to the point of death.

CHAPTER XVI

NEAR DEATH
1921-1922

Archbishop Hanna was now confronted with a most serious problem. The Brothers had given their formal notification that they were going to give up St. Vincent's. The Dominican Sisters had agreed to take over only the domestic work and that not until August of the following year. Therefore, there was the problem of getting teachers for the school. The outlook here was most dismal, for the problem described by the Brothers as affecting them, also applied to other religious groups. The teacher shortage was acute among all the religious communities.

The solution found by the Archbishop was certainly to prove unique. Whether he intended it to be a permanent or a temporary solution we do not know for certain. Within a month after the Brothers' formal notice had been given, the Archbishop approached the Superintendent of Public Schools of Marin County. This certainly was an unprecedented step, and one which was to cause further complications.

Mr. James B. Davidson, the Superintendent of Marin County Schools, proved to be St. Vincent's benefactor during these months. Having accepted the Archbishop's invitation to take over the school at St. Vincent's, Mr. Davidson at once proceeded to work out the problems that arose. First of all, St. Vincent's was located in the Dixie school district, which possessed a small rural school of one room and less than ten pupils. St. Vincent's was now adding approximately four hundred pupils to the school roll of the district. The only possible place for classes to be held was in St. Vincent's own buildings, which in itself presented a problem.

In a letter to Mr. Davidson from Mr. Will C. Wood, the State Superintendent of Public Instruction, the solution to the location problem was as follows:

> *"The orphanage has no separate buildings available for school purposes. It appears that the only buildings available are wings of the main building of the Institution. These are not in a good state of repair; in*

fact, they have seen practically all their usefulness. However, they might be made available for instruction purposes. I am of the opinion that any plan involving the permanent use of the wings of the orphanage for school purposes would be challenged and that school funds would be held up because people cannot readily understand that a non-sectarian school can be conducted in a sectarian orphanage. If the buildings were separate, the distinction could be readily understood. It should be distinctly understood that the use of the orphanage buildings for school purposes is only temporary and that new school buildings separate from the orphanage building must be provided within a reasonable time."

As a result of this cooperation between the two Superintendents it was decided that the classroom wing of St. Vincent's should be rented by the State. It was expressly understood that "such school shall be exclusively under the control of the board of trustees of the Dixie school district and pupils enrolled therein shall, during the regular school hours, be exclusively under the jurisdiction of the public school authorities. The course of study pursued in said school shall be the course of study for the public schools of Marin County and the textbooks those prescribed by law. No sectarian or denominational doctrine shall be taught in said school."

The second problem was the financing of this school. In a memorandum prepared by Mr. Davidson in December, 1921, he outlined this problem:

"The Dixie school district in which St. Vincent's is located has no funds available to maintain school during the remainder of this year, and no apportionment of public funds can be made available until the school has been maintained 160 days during a school year."

On this basis, the daily attendance for the remainder of the school year would give the Dixie district a right to State funds in the following year. But, even this would hardly suffice to pay the teachers salaries, for, as Mr. Wood pointed out: "In view of the fact that the type of boy represented at St. Vincent's demands a strong teacher, I do not believe that satisfactory teachers could be employed without liberal supplementing of State and County funds." The problem was solved by the Archbishop, who volunteered to pay the salaries for the six months period under question. The amount estimated by Mr. Davidson and agreed upon by the Archbishop was $9,600.

The third problem, the one on which Mr. Davidson himself worked very conscientiously, was that of getting sufficient and qualified teachers. To realize fully the task that lay before him, one must remember that this was the month of October. All the good available teachers were already employed for the school year that had begun in September. To find ten good teachers now was a giant undertaking. Mr. Davidson commenced by writing all the normal schools in the state. He addressed letters to the Teachers Colleges in Chico, San Diego, Arcata, San Jose, Santa Barbara and the University of California in Berkeley. Teachers he did find, but for the most part inexperienced young men and women. The more he pondered the problem the clearer became the obvious solution. Mr. Davidson then made the big decision to ask some of the best teachers in his school system to accept the assignments at St. Vincent's and he would put the new inexperienced people in their places. In that way he could scatter the new teachers among various schools rather than concentrate all of them in one school. In that way too, he could insure for St. Vincent's the best teachers available. This decision brought with it another worry. On December 3, 1921, the State Superintendent wrote to Mr. Davidson concerning his decision:

> "Since leaving you yesterday I have given thought to possible complications growing out of the plan for St. Vincent's. The thing that brought it most strikingly home to me was the plan to take people out of teaching positions and put them in the proposed school. I think this should be done if we are to secure good teachers, but I should feel quite blameable if after these teachers had resigned and accepted a place at St. Vincent's, a legal point were raised and an adverse opinion on the legal status of the plan were rendered. Moreover, I should feel culpable if the Archbishop, assuming that the matter could be fully settled by us, were induced to expend a considerable sum for the school, only to find that legal difficulties prevented carrying out the plan of public support.
>
> In consequence, I have decided to submit the entire matter to the Attorney General for opinion. I do not see that the submission of the matter need interfere with plans for the school. However, I believe that all teachers selected should be fully informed concerning the legal status of the plan. I am sure that all of us will feel much more easy in mind if the legal points are cleared up now rather than later."

Word of the plan for the school leaked out. When it reached the ears of the Brothers at St. Vincent's, the reaction was almost explosive. These Brothers were most devoted to their charge and deeply interested in their work. The very thought of having to give up the institution grieved them, but the thought that someone else had been asked to teach in the school while they were still in the institution caused them untold sorrow. Evidently the Archbishop was willing to release the teaching Brothers as soon as possible, but he had expected the other Brothers to remain until the arrival of the Sisters in August, 1922. But this was not according to the Brothers' liking. In a letter to the Archbishop on November 25, 1921, Brother Joseph, the Visitor, explained it as follows: "The Brothers have petitioned me so to arrange it that we go out in a body; they were a unit in opposing the plan to give up the classes at one time and the management at another; they seemed to me to be hurt."

This upset state of affairs was to continue for another month. The Archbishop was unable to give the Brothers a definite answer until the legal question had been settled.

It was on December 21, 1921 that U. S. Webb, the Attorney General of the State of California, rendered his opinion that there was no legal objection to the setting up of the school as proposed by the State and County Superintendents. It was, therefore, definitely decided that St. Vincent's would become a public school on January 2, 1922.

The die was cast. The Marin County School Department was ready to take over the school; and the Brothers, who saw in this the complete undoing of all their labors, had given their ultimatum. This presented to the Archbishop a problem that over-shadowed all other difficulties. Since the Dominican Sisters could not come until August, 1922, who was to run the institution during those eight months? The school was a minor problem now because it was in the hands of capable people. But the care of the boys was a major problem indeed. The answer to this too was obvious. Lay help would have to be hired to replace the Brothers. But the Brothers worked around the clock, seven days a week. To replace fourteen Brothers would take twice as many lay people who could not be expected to devote as many hours as a religious would give. Secondly, these people would have to have adequate salaries. The Brothers had labored for no salary, devoting themselves to their work without personal recompense. To pay salaries to a staff sufficient to replace the Brothers would raise the cost of maintaining St. Vincent's for the year 1922 to staggering proportions. The whole future of St. Vincent's was at stake now, not just the classroom situation.

The Brothers were under orders from their superiors. They began to prepare to leave. The task of replacing Brother Vellesian[19] with a new Director was the Archbishop's problem. It seemed as if the task of obtaining a new bookkeeper would also be a difficult problem. The Brothers, in summing up the requirements for this wrote:

> *"This man is to replace Brother Dionysius, who occupied, from the administration viewpoint, the most important, because the most minute and varied, position in the institution. He must be able to meet people, to pay wages, bills, etc. An attempt at a statement of this office as carried out by Brother Dionysius is impossible."*

It took just such an occasion as this to bring to attention the valuable work of one so faithful as Brother Dionysius.

A job also impossible to describe had been done on the farm for twenty-seven years by Brother Vincent. He had come to St. Vincent's shortly after Brother Azary's work there had been completed. For all those years he had supervised the plowing, the seeding, the haying, the stock raising, the dairying, vegetable growing, fruit raising, pruning, etc. He had taken special care of those older boys who worked in these various jobs on the farm. There was now needed a new foreman. William Marsh and George Haves were farm workers, but it would take an exceptional man to be the foreman.

In charge of the boys, Thomas Phelan was appointed Head Prefect. He would have full authority over the boys during the hours out of school. To assist him were Thomas Doyle, Michael Flanagan, and Sam McKee. Mrs. Phelan was to continue in charge of the little boys, a position she had occupied for several years. Ray McIntyre was the Band Master.

The husband and wife combination was not limited to the Phelans. Manuel Velasquez had proven himself a very reliable shoemaker and he also was in charge of the clothes room. His wife was in charge of the chicken yard. Mr. McKee, the Prefect, was also married. His wife worked in the clothes room and assisted Mrs. Phelan in the care of the small boys.

One other woman on the staff besides Miss MacMillan, the nurse, was Mrs. Mary Zazzi. She had the care of the pantry, the dining rooms, and the chapel. The Brothers described her as "competent, certainly earns her salary ($40.00) and is a treasure to the institution."

The laundryman, Joseph Schneider, was described as a faithful and competent workman, whose salary Brother Dionysius recommended should be raised to sixty dollars. Besides there was the engineer, William Littleford, described as "an expert, whose high ($150.00) salary is explained by the fact that the boilermakers, whom we had so often to call in for expensive repairs, recommended an expert, claiming that no ordinary mechanic could keep the engines up." There was the plumber, Frank Watson, the carpenter, Thomas Lawton, the head janitor, Clarence Love, and the night watchman, Stanley Siligant.

The largest number of employees was necessary in the kitchen. Here there were a baker, a head cook, a second cook, an employees' cook, a steward, and a dishwasher. All these employees, so very necessary in order to run the institution without the Brothers, would receive salaries totaling over $1,800 a month. This was to be even more costly for the eight month period than the salaries of the public school teachers.

Lastly the Brothers made provision for the teaching of religion, their own first devotion, which was now put out of the classroom and the school hours. The religious instruction would be given every night, except Sunday, at 7:00 P.M. by Father McKeon, the Chaplain since 1916, assisted by Mr. Phelan, Mr. Doyle, Mr. Flanagan and Mrs. Phelan.

As the Brothers completed these arrangements in preparation for their leaving, Mr. Davidson was completing his arrangements for taking over the school. A meeting of the Board of Trustees of the Dixie School District was held at St. Vincent's on December 23, 1921, and the teachers were appointed for the term beginning January 2, 1922. One of those present at that meeting was Mr. Bernard Hoffman, a devoted trustee even to this day. On the same day as this meeting, the Attorney General's opinion was received in the office of the Archbishop. Arrangements were now completed.

However, the school did not commence January second. On that date Mr. Davidson wrote to the State Superintendent that they were still short two teachers but they hoped to begin on the ninth.

Even the man selected by Mr. Davidson to be Principal was at the last moment unable to get a release from his school. Then Mr. Davidson secured Mr. Leo Taylor from the Golden Gate Junior High in Oakland. The school commenced on January ninth as planned with the following teachers under Mr. Taylor:

> Clarence S. Pearce, Mrs. Viola Kelley, Warren Allison, Mrs. Mary Mc-Curdy, Miss Frances Hrubetz, Miss Ellen Redding, Mrs. Eva Winkel, Miss Julia Arges, and Mrs. Agnes Boulter.

Through the efforts of Mr. Davidson, a Manual Training Shop was opened with Mr. L. Gowan as the instructor. Archbishop Hanna paid the bill of $500 for equipment.

Four days after the new school opened, the Archbishop appointed the successor of Brother Vellesian, a selection which was to be the most fortunate in the entire life of St. Vincent's, and which was to save it from the death struggle into which it had just been plunged.

Chapter XVII

REBIRTH
1922-1925

The new Director was Father Francis P. McElroy, a priest most eminently fitted for the task that now lay before him. Born in San Francisco on September 27, 1881, he had received his early education at St. Joseph's School at Tenth and Howard Streets. In 1891 he went to St. Patrick's Seminary in Menlo Park where he spent twelve years, receiving his high school and college education and pursuing his theological studies in preparation for the priesthood. He was ordained on June 21, 1910. His assignments included All Saints Church in Hayward in 1911; Sacred Heart Church in Oakland in 1912; St. Patrick's Church in San Jose in 1915, and St. Raphael's Church in San Rafael on September 29, 1915. During his three years at San Rafael he served as Chaplain at San Quentin Prison, an experience which, no doubt, gave him valuable insight into young men's problems. On February 29, 1918 he was transferred to Sacred Heart Church in San Francisco. It was while there that he gathered around himself boys who, rather than going to school, were working for a living, due to the fact that they had no home of their own. Father McElroy had discovered, perhaps at San Quentin, that such young men without the security of home often fell into difficulties which brought them eventually to prison.

In 1919, Father McElroy bought a house at 832 Fell Street, around the corner from Sacred Heart Church. Here he gathered these young men whom he had been helping. The house was known as the San Francisco Working Boys' Club. The Archbishop officially appointed Father McElroy as the Director in June, 1919. Slowly his life work was beginning to take shape. When confronted with the enormous problem of St. Vincent's in 1921, the Archbishop began to look for someone capable of handling the situation. His choice fell on Father McElroy. On January 13, 1922 the official appointment was made. He transferred his residence to St. Vincent's and there with Father McKeon he watched and observed as the school year progressed under the new program. Meanwhile in his mind he was formulating new plans. When the school year closed in June the teachers went on vacation. No one knew for sure what the program would be in the Fall. All that was certain was that the Dominican Sisters were coming to do the domestic work. They had accepted the Archbishop's invitation shortly before the Brothers' formal resignation had been published. On September 16, 1921 Mother Pia, the Prioress General had written to the Vicar General:

> *"The Councillors have decided that we should do the utmost, even at the cost of sacrifice, for the sake of helping the Most Rev. Archbishop in his project with the Boys' Home. Considering that the boys will attend the public school to be erected for them, we are willing to furnish ten Sisters (although twenty would be necessary for the undertaking) to take charge of the Home after August 4, 1922, stipulating however for a trial of five years."*

This last condition recalls a similar one for three months made by the Dominican Sisters of Benicia in 1868. They stayed twenty-six years. The five years of the Dominican Sisters of Mission San Jose have already expanded into thirty-three years. Mother Pia visited St. Vincent's during the summer of 1922. In the course of her visit she was shown the school building. For the first time she suddenly realized what having a public school on the grounds meant. In every classroom the walls were bare of any crucifix, holy picture or other religious symbol. These had been removed as soon as the building became State property. This was too much for the staunch Catholic heart of Mother Pia. In an inspired moment that made her the second mother of St. Vincent's, she turned and announced that at any cost she would have teachers for the school the following August. Father McElroy in grateful remembrance for this act later dedicated one of the new buildings to the memory of this Mother of the new St. Vincent's.

It was on Monday, August 7, 1922 that Mother Seraphina, Mother Pia's assistant, brought the first Sisters, Sister Anastasia, who was to be the Superior, and Sister Sebastian. On the following day seven more arrived. They were Sisters Emygdia, Hyacinth, Wilhelmina, Osanna, Felicia, Cornelia and Petronilla. On the ninth the last two, Sisters Innocentia and Petrina, arrived. These eleven formed the first Community.

On the following Sunday the Sisters fully realized what had happened in the eight months since the Brothers left. The three hundred boys arrived for Sunday Mass in their overalls! The "well shod and very tidy" Sunday dress under the Brothers was no longer a reality. The Sisters, as soon as they were themselves settled, immediately attacked the clothing situation and their description of the condition of the children's clothing after these eight months is indeed amazing. While the Sisters were working at the clothing, Mother Seraphina was preparing for the opening of the school. On August 16, 1922 all was in readiness. A procession was formed. A child from each class carried a crucifix and in a grateful and prayerful manner the crucifix was enthroned in each classroom; St. Vincent's was again a Catholic school.

The following teachers had been engaged:

Sister Anastasia in the 8th Grade
Miss Ellen Redding was retained in the 7th Grade
Miss McCauley taught the 6th
Miss Spottiswood was in the 5th
Miss Elizabeth Smith took care of the 4th
Mrs. Hamilton had the 3rd
Sister Cornelia taught the 2nd
Sister Osanna had the 1st.

Thus the school opened with three Sisters and five lay teachers and 298 boys. Within two months a vast difference was noticeable in the institution. Nothing of course could be done about the buildings. They were old and falling apart. But the Sisters worked day and night to give each boy a complete outfit of new clothing. The triumphal day came on Sunday, October 1, the Patronal feast of the Chapel of the Holy Rosary. On that day the Sisters and Father McKeon were most encouraged when they saw all the boys neatly dressed at Mass with very many of them receiving Communion on the occasion. The great satisfaction was in the knowledge that each child present had a complete new wardrobe.

The next event of importance in 1922 occurred on December 1st. On that day Father McKeon was transferred by the Archbishop to Sausalito after six years of devoted service to St. Vincent's. On the same day came the new assistant, Father Peter Weber. The appointments of Father McElroy and Father Weber to St. Vincent's must certainly have been divinely inspired because this priestly team brought a new life to St. Vincent's. Father Weber, by his background, was prepared to give the institution a unique type of service. He was a farmer by birth and by experience. Born in Gridley, California on November 30, 1881, the son of Peter and Mary Weber, he was acquainted with agricultural life from childhood. He attended the public schools of Butte County from 1889 to 1899, and Gridley High School during the years 1899 and 1900. In this latter year he entered St. Patrick's Seminary in Menlo Park. Twelve years later, on June 22, 1912 he was ordained a priest.

For the next three years the farm life was forgotten as he fulfilled priestly duties in Tomales from July, 1912 to January, 1913, and in Napa from January, 1913 to November, 1914. Then began his association with Father Crowley; Father Weber was appointed Assistant Director of the Youths Directory. In the course of six months, Father Crowley discovered Father Weber's knowledge of and love for the soil. He saw in this young priest the answer to his problems at St. Joseph's Agricultural Institute, a farm project of the Youths Directory which Father Crowley had given to the care of the Brothers of Mary. Father Weber was therefore appointed to the Rutherford farm in June, 1915. For the next two and a half years, Father Weber had invaluable experience in teaching farm work to boys. Once again he got the feel of the plow and the tractor. He saw the soil produce under the skill of cultivation. It all came to an apparent end in December, 1917, when the Archbishop transferred him to Mission Dolores in San Francisco. Here for the next five years Father Weber performed priestly duties with the care and exactness so characteristic of him.

When the Brothers left St. Vincent's in August, 1922, the need of a skillful man to succeed Brother Vincent on the farm was pointed out. Father McKeon had filled in as foreman during the following three months. Suddenly someone thought of the skill and background of Father Weber. If anyone could manage St. Vincent's farm and help get the institution on an economical basis, it should be Father Weber. Indeed his appointment in December, 1922 was a brilliant stroke of genius.

For the next eighteen years he led a hidden life. Hardly anyone saw him, but everyone heard of the marvels this truly humble man worked. He came to be hailed as "one of the greatest practical farmers of California". The *Monitor* of November 30, 1940 describes his activities thus:

"Father Weber grew the fruit and taught the Sisters of St. Dominic how to can them. He raised the beef and pork and fowl. He delivered the milk and eggs, foods beyond all imagining. It is a development comparable to a medieval Benedictine Abbey. He directed older boys in building; he reclaimed land from the bay."

Day after day Father Weber's life was filled with work. He always said the earliest Mass. His prayers and his breakfast followed. Then the priestly dress was changed to boots and khaki. With the arrival of the earliest workman Father Weber was on hand. He outlined the day's operations. He drove the tractors, directed the farming in every form. Each night he was the first to bed and as regular as a clock.

Under his care, St. Vincent's became almost self supporting as far as food was concerned. Except for lamb, since sheep ruin pasture land, Father Weber increased the beef herds, the pigs, the chicken ranch to such numbers that he produced all the beef, the pork, the bacon and the chickens needed for food. He bred and raised his own calves. He increased the cows to sufficient numbers that there was ample milk on the table twice a day for three hundred boys. He turned the reclaimed lands into hay and alfalfa sufficient to feed his stock. The orchards bore enough fruit that with the hard work of the Sisters during canning season there was abundant fruit of every description for dessert throughout the long winter months. Eggs and cream and butter abounded. The prosperous condition of St. Vincent's farm today is due to the work of Father Weber during those eighteen years. Of course, this was not all accomplished at once, nor in several seasons of planting and harvesting. But slowly and surely he built up the farm to its present state.

While Father Weber labored to feed the boys and feed them as they had never before been fed, Father McElroy was concerned about their housing. He began to make plans for rebuilding St. Vincent's. His plan was to obtain permission from the Archbishop and the Pastors to go around the Archdiocese on Sundays, preach in the various parishes and collect funds for the building project. The genius of Father McElroy began to unfold as he stood Sunday after Sunday in the pulpit and told his story. Billfolds and check books were opened as he opened the hearts of his listeners. The money began to come in. In his preaching the poor heard him and gave what they could, but the rich heard him too and gave of their abundance. Two such interested listeners were Mrs. Julia Babcock of San Rafael and Mr. James Walsh of San Francisco. These came forth and pledged such large donations that Father McElroy was able to begin to build at once. He engaged Mr. Leo Mitchell as his architect. Then Father McElroy told him what he wanted. The ideas that were to be realized in the new St. Vincent's began to unfold.

The new St. Vincent's was to be a departure from the old institutional form. The best ideas of the cottage system would be incorporated into the new building. St. Vincent's would use the unit system, the same as the cottage system, but without separating the buildings. Each unit would house thirty boys. There would be a living room equipped with a fireplace, opening off a porch. Behind it would be a washroom equipped with lockers, sink, toilets and shower. Upstairs would be a dormitory capable of holding thirty beds with windows on both sides and a room for a house-' mother at one end. The plans for the first new building were beginning to take shape. It would include a spacious auditorium two stories high, with stage, gallery and projection room. Attached to this would be three living units accommodating ninety boys.

On December 8, 1923 the ceremony of breaking ground was held. All the boys were in attendance; the Band was on hand with appropriate numbers. Mrs. Babcock was present and turned the first shovelful of earth. The happiness in the heart of Father McElroy abounded. During the next month, the old infirmary cottage was removed and the north front wing occupied by the Student Brothers during the years of the Training School was torn down. On January 7, 1924, work began on the new unit. The auditorium bears the plaque "William Babcock Memorial". Two of the living units are called the "James Walsh Home" and the "Archbishop Hanna Home". But because through the years these units were to house the middle-sized boys, ages eight and nine, the whole building came to be known as the "Middle Dormitory" and to this day it bears that name rather than the names of its chief benefactors.

Meanwhile progress was being made in the school. When it had closed for the term in June, 1923, there had been 337 boys. Thirteen had completed the eighth grade. Father McElroy was then faced with the problem of what to do. Would he follow the policy of his predecessors for the past sixty-eight years and "farm out" these boys; or would he abandon this practice and try to give them a high school education or at least part of one? Not knowing what it would bring, but feeling reluctant to turn out boys at fourteen, at a most important period in their lives, Father McElroy decided to hold on to them for at least one more year. Therefore a ninth grade was added.

For this new school term in August, 1923, there were four Sisters and two lay women. A man had been engaged to teach the combined eighth and ninth grades.

Just four months after the construction of the new building had commenced, Father McElroy ordered the second building torn down. The wrecking began on April 28, 1924. Great must have been the joy in the hearts of the boys to be able to wreck something with permission. Under watchful eyes the old three story building began to come down. Then the concrete was poured. A second new building was under way before the first was half finished.

On August 9, 1924 Sister Loyola joined the community of Sisters and three days later Mother Pia sent a new Superior in the person of Sister Hedwig. When school opened a few days later there were no lay women, just the Sisters and two men in the upper grades.

The day of days came on December 15, 1924, for on that occasion the Babcock unit was blessed by Father McElroy, assisted by Father Weber. That afternoon Sister Sebastian and her brood of boys moved into their new $90,000 home. Two evenings later, on December 17, 1924, the new auditorium was used for the first time for the weekly moving picture. The new St. Vincent's was no longer a dream: it had been truly reborn.

First new building in 1924, auditorium and three living units.

Second building completed in 1925 contains three living units.

CHAPTER XVIII

DIAMOND JUBILEE YEARS
1925 - 1930

St. Vincent's had scarcely begun the seventieth year of its life when it lost its second mother. The beloved Mother Pia, whose willingness to sacrifice at any cost to save St. Vincent's, died on February 8, 1925. It was this fact that inspired Father McElroy to dedicate one of the living units in the second building now nearing completion to her memory. Another unit bears the plaque, "Achille Roos Home". This building, like the first one, was not destined to be called by either of its dedicated names. Because it has housed the little ones, ages six and seven, it has been known as the "Little Dormitory". The dedication date was set for May 10, 1925. Archbishop Hanna agreed to bless this unit himself. Father McElroy, who began to show his talent for showmanship, arranged an elaborate outdoor ceremony. The day dawned stormy and windy, but as the time for the ceremony approached, the skies cleared, although the wind continued to blow. The dedication took place as scheduled. The band awaited the Archbishop in the front. As his car drove up, the musicians burst forth into martial airs. The boys then accompanied the guest of honor to the new unit and occupied their places, sitting on the hillside close by. The Archbishop blessed the building and then spoke to the boys. Benediction of the Blessed Sacrament followed, but it was so windy that the candles did not remain lighted. That evening this second building, composed of three living units capable of accommodating ninety boys, was occupied. The entire north wing of St. Vincent's had been replaced.

The school year closed on June 26, 1925, with three hundred ninety-four boys, thirteen being graduates from the eighth grade. This fact presented once again the necessity of a major decision. Not only were there these thirteen ready for the ninth grade, but there was a similar number of boys now ready for the tenth grade. Would these last be kept or sent away? The financial arrangement pertaining to these boys had changed in the past few years. State aid was no longer given directly, but rather to the counties and to individual families through the aid to needy children programs. Also the age had been raised to sixteen. With this assurance of support there was no longer the grave financial risk involved in keeping these older boys. Therefore Father McElroy resolved to add a tenth grade. However, still influenced by the idea of giving boys in this age bracket a so-called "useful" trade, the Director decided his ninth and tenth grades would compose a commercial high school. Therefore, when school opened in August, 1926, the new high school department taught such subjects as business English, typing, shorthand, bookkeeping, and arithmetic, with, of course, a class in religion. A few of these older boys, not fitted by talent or inclination for such a course were given to Father Weber, who put them to work on the farm or on the grounds and taught them many practical lessons that fitted them for a future agricultural life. There were three hundred one pupils on the opening day of school. The teachers were Sisters Hedwig, Flavia, Francisca, Constantia, and Agnes Mary. Mr. Fitzgibbons, Mr. Dattner, and Mr. O'Brien taught the upper classes.

In October, 1925, Father McElroy had faced the future and found the outlook dismal. The job of rebuilding the south wing of St. Vincent's seemed colossal. The problem, a financial one, seemed doubly difficult because there was no second Mrs. Babcock available. But Father McElroy found a second benefactress, this time a heavenly one, in St. Therese, the Little Flower, who had been recently canonized. Her story had impressed Father McElroy. He decided to put the new building program under her care. The priests, Sisters, and boys began a novena on October 21, 1925. A few days later, there came a check for $1,000, and within a week the sum of $57,000. The next new building was beginning to seem possible. The decision was made that the novena should be held every month beginning on the First Friday and continuing for the nine days. Father McElroy was now so encouraged that he ordered Father McKinnon's building across the east end, and the east end of the south wing torn down in preparation for another building. On March 19, 1926, work commenced on the third building, a duplicate of the second, with three living units capable of housing ninety boys. A great deal of grading was necessary now and in the future, as this new south wing would be built farther south than

The forms for the second building with old south wing in background.

Old south wing gone; forms for third building started.

Third building completed.

Old Administration Wing Stands Alone.

the old one, thus making the interior garden much wider. The sound of blasting caused much excitement among the boys and often made teaching school a problem for the Sisters. All that was left now of the old St. Vincent's was the chapel, the old administration building, and the front south wing where the Sisters were living.

The month of May, 1926 brought two events of interest. Mr. Flannigan, the Prefect since the departure of the Christian Brothers, met with an accident. Not thinking it serious, he had simply gone to bed in his own room for a few days. On May 25, it became apparent that his condition was indeed serious. He was sent to the hospital where he became unconscious on Tuesday night. The following day he died. In grateful remembrance for his devoted service, St. Vincent's Chapel was the scene of his funeral. Burial was in San Rafael.

On May 27, 1926, Archbishop Hanna came to administer Confirmation. Sixty-eight boys, dressed in white shirts, white pants, and white shoes were presented to the Archbishop. Their sponsor was Doctor Leo Boyle. This Confirmation reveals two facts concerning Father McElroy. From the very beginning, he realized that every boy, whether he be an orphan or not likes to dress up on occasions. His first venture, therefore, was to dress up the excellent choir. For this he put his relatives, his friends, everyone he could find, to work. His own sister, Mrs. Thomas Manning, was put in charge. The cassocks were a deep purple, with red cuffs and a large red bow tie set off by a starched "Buster Brown" collar. A white surplice completed the outfit. Over one hundred sets were made to fit boys six to sixteen. This choir dress is still in use, and the pride and joy radiating from the faces of the boys when they are all dressed up is evident manifestation that Father McElroy knew what he was doing. The Band boys, too, were dressed up, but their uniform was to be changed in later years to the present one. The occasions of First Communion and Confirmation were celebrated with the boys dressed in spotless white, a uniform still worn on these memorable occasions. Father McElroy's philosophy about St. Vincent's was becoming evident. He felt that if boys were put in an atmosphere of elegance and beauty they would in some manner attempt to measure up. If their surroundings were dull and uninviting, they too would never aspire to anything refined or good. This philosophy explains why he selected the beautiful mission style architecture of the buildings. It also explains the elaborate gardens that are enclosed by the buildings. For this, Father McElroy put his own brother to work. Skilled in the art of landscaping, Will McElroy selected an Italian formal garden as the design for the rear court between the newly completed buildings. The older boys poured the concrete blocks which were used to form the walks that surround the garden. A beautifully ornamented fountain graced the center. Hundreds of plants of every kind were bought, donated, and begged, and were eventually transplanted into the new garden. St. Vincent's was becoming a place of beauty.

The second quality exhibited by Father McElroy was his ability to surround himself with faithful employees, whose work became a devotion, and whose loyalty persevered many years after he himself was gone. In 1924, he added to his list of employees the name of "Thomas Ducey, Carpenter". For the next twenty-eight years this man was part of the life of St. Vincent's, first as carpenter, later as ranch foreman. One of the first tasks imposed on "Tom" was the fitting up of a new school. With the razing of the south wing early in 1926, the classrooms were destroyed. Father McElroy now made a radical change. Since six living units were completed on the north side, the three huge dormitories in the new Christian Brothers' building of 1912 were only partly occupied. The remaining boys were now moved out and Mr. Ducey and his helpers began to construct classrooms within the space of the three dormitories. The two washrooms were torn out; partitions were erected, providing space for twelve rooms. Hundreds of panes of glass were used for the top of the partitions which ran down the entire length of the building, providing light for the central hallway. The construction of the Babcock unit had eliminated the infirmary cottage; the destruction of the south wing had removed the remaining infirmary facilities. Therefore, Father McElroy put to use the "half story" of the 1912 building. The top floor provided a fine infirmary. Here too a complete dental office was set up and the services of another faithful friend of St. Vincent's were obtained in the person of Dr. Leo Boyle, who still serves as the school dentist every Friday in the year. Until this time, boys who needed dental attention were taken to San Rafael. But this was only when they needed attention. No preventive work had been done. With the arrival of Dr. Boyle, a complete program of dental care was inaugurated, including examination, fillings, extractions, and referrals for corrective dental work.

The reconstruction continued through the year 1926. In the fall the new building was completed. Into this moved the big boys, a fact which gave it the name of "Big Dormitory". There were now just three old buildings left; Father Lootens' wing which was the administration building, the front south wing where the Sisters were living, and the chapel built by Father Croke in 1881. These would be next if the money came in. The monthly novena to St. Therese continued; the money kept coming in from countless benefactors. In July the Sisters moved out of their house and the wrecking crews took over. On August 27, 1926, the last of that old building was gone. But the next new part of the south wing could not be constructed unless the chapel came down. With the new south wing further out than the old one, the chapel blocked possible construction. To tear this down would present a real problem because a church was needed. Father McElroy found the solution to that problem also. The auditorium would serve as an excellent temporary chapel. With the suddenness of such a decision that was so characteristic of him, everyone was expected to work at once. The day was St. Patrick's Day, March 17, 1927. In the auditorium carpets were laid, side altars were put in place, statues transferred, and the temporary main altar fixed and dressed. By four o'clock that afternoon, all was in readiness to transfer the Blessed Sacrament from the old to the new, temporary chapel. The boys were assembled and lined up from the old church door to the auditorium. The older boys who were doing so much of the work carried the canopy as Father McElroy, in procession, carried the Blessed Sacrament to its new home. As soon as he reached the new chapel, Father McElroy gave Benediction. Two days later, on the feast of St. Joseph, March 19, Mass was offered for the first time in the new chapel.

Work went on, stripping the interior of the old church. On April 11, the workers were ready to take down the steeple. As they climbed about it, they found it to be very shaky. After nearly fifty years of withstanding the strong winds of the winter months, it was no wonder that it was shaky. All was in readiness. Everyone was uneasy. The long ropes were taut; the tractors pulled. The tower screeched and shook. Then it tumbled down without mishap.

An old landmark was gone. It would be two years before a new tower would take its place. Only one building remained, the old administration wing. It too came down under the hands of the wreckers. Not a trace of the old wooden buildings was left.

On April 22, 1927, grief came upon Father McElroy, caused by the death of his mother. Quite shaken by it, it became obvious that he was also tired from all the reconstruction and fund raising work. He needed a vacation. Archbiship Hanna invited Father McElroy to accompany him to Rome. Departure was delayed a few days in order that Father McElroy might attend an event on May 4, 1927, in the Civic Auditorium in San Francisco in which his vested choir boys sang. Five days later, on May 9, 1927, he left for Rome.

During Father McElroy's absence, one event took place which is tersely recorded in the Sisters' Annals as follows: "June 22, 1927. Twenty-three boys came to us from the Youths Directory. Fire destroyed their home." In these few words is told the destruction of Father Crowley's work. In a few months, the shock was to cause his death. The new St. Vincent's had a chance to express its gratitude to Father Crowley by accepting some of his homeless boys. A month after Father Crowley's death, Father McElroy was appointed Director of the Youths Directory on March 23, 1928.

Father McElroy returned from his vacation on August 14, 1927. School opened two days later with two hundred sixty boys. Construction had meanwhile been progressing on the new administration wing which was to house the Sisters on the second floor. On January 20, 1928, Father McElroy and Father Weber moved into rooms near the auditorium while a house for themselves was being moved into its new location. By March, 1928, the new administration building was ready for occupancy. The new furnishings arrived on March 12, and on the following day the Sisters moved into their new convent and the new offices were occupied.

When school opened on August 20, 1928, there were three hundred twenty boys. The construction work had started on the last wing. It would match the first unit. There would be two living units and a magnificent new chapel, which would be the crowning work of the reconstructed St. Vincent's. Designed by Leo Mitchel, with Leibert and Trobock as contractors, the new chapel and living units began to rise. In grateful appreciation for his devoted service as architect, Father McElroy named one of the new living units the "Leo Mitchel Home". The magnificent new chapel, titled "Queen of the Holy Rosary", was the gift of an anonymous donor, known only to Father McElroy. Designed to seat four hundred, the Italian Renaissance-mission style chapel stands as one of the beautiful churches of the archdiocese. The beautiful stained glass windows, depicting many of the "childhood" scenes of the life of Christ and the mysteries of the rosary were imported. The white marble altar and statues are unmatched in their beauty. Father McElroy left nothing out to make this chapel the crowning point in the newly built St. Vincent's. Although completed in 1929, the dedication was postponed to coincide with the Diamond Jubilee to be celebrated in the summer of 1930.

Meanwhile, surprising news came on April 15, 1930. In recognition of his work, Pope Pius XI had named Father McElroy a monsignor. This news was hailed with extreme joy by all. A wonderful work and a wonderful man had been recognized. On June 7, 1930, the Monitor carried the announcement of the Diamond Jubilee of St. Vincent's and the dedication of the new chapel to be held on June 29, 1930, exactly forty-nine years after the dedication of the old church.

"St. Vincent's to Observe 75th Jubilee" — "Archbishop Hanna to Dedicate New Chapel — 20,000 Expected to Attend". So ran the headlines. Father John Cassin, the retired Pastor of Santa Rosa, assistant at St. Vincent's in 1876, was to be the celebrant of the Mass. Sharing in the honors would be Father James Newell, O.P., a priest who had assisted at the dedication of the first chapel erected by Father Lootens. Archbishop Hanna would preach the sermon, and Bishop John J. Cantwell of Los Angeles would give Benediction. Father Edgar Boyle was in charge of the ninety voice boys' choir which would sing at the dedication. Father McElroy would be invested in his robes as a Monsignor. St. Vincent's Band would hold a concert before and after the ceremony.

Such were the announcements pertaining to the Jubilee-Dedication day. June 29, 1930 dawned a beautiful day. Thousands of people arrived for the occasion. Two thousand automobiles drove in the lane that leads to St. Vincent's. An unforgettable celebration was held on this occasion. St. Vincent's formally began a new era in its long life.

Rt. Rev. Francis P. McElroy, The Father of the new St. Vincent's. The Thirteenth Director—1922-1943.

CHAPTER XIX

TRANSFORMATION
1930 - 1943

Externally, St. Vincent's had been transformed into a place of beauty. But men have learned through experience that one cannot judge by externals only. A beautiful school building does not necessarily imply that a good education is imparted within its walls. A beautiful institution like St. Vincent's must be internally as excellent as it appears if it is to do a real service. Since Monsignor McElroy realized this fact fully, he carried out an internal transformation at St. Vincent's while he was changing its exterior appearance. His first departure from the old system was to drop the use of such words as "Orphanage", "Asylum", "Inmates". He renamed the institution "St. Vincent's School for Boys", although the old corporation title still remained unchanged. It is quite obvious why the Director felt the word "Orphanage" was a misnomer. There were practically no more orphans at St. Vincent's. Times had changed, industrial accidents had been reduced, and new social welfare practices had developed which favored foster home care for orphans, thus eliminating orphans from St. Vincent's rolls. The most significant change effected by Monsignor McElroy was the decision that no more delinquents would be accepted at St. Vincent's. The policy originated by him still perseveres to this day. St. Vincent's was to be a home for boys who were forced temporarily to be placed outside their own family circle for reasons of illness in the family, death of one parent, divorce or other similar factors which made a boy a dependent.

This change in the admission policy was to have its effect on the whole school, on its aims and objectives, and most of all, on what it could accomplish. But there were other changes which also had tremendous influence on the welfare of the boys. In 1933 the Catholic Youth Organization, popularly known as the C.Y.O., expanded itself westward from Chicago where it had been founded. A program for youth, of a religious, intellectual, and social nature, it stressed athletics as a means of keeping boys together, actively

occupied in a constructive manner. When it was decided to start
the program in the Archdiocese, Archbishop Hanna put Monsignor McElroy in charge of the C.Y.O. and left it to his genius to
organize it throughout the Archdiocese. For the next three years
until slowed by illness, Monsignor McElroy turned his energy into
the development of the C.Y.O. program.

First to benefit by it was St. Vincent's. Teams were organized
in basketball and baseball, meeting the C.Y.O. requirements.
Equipment was bought and donated. Since the C.Y.O. colors were
green and white, St. Vincent's boys now donned green and white
basketball and baseball uniforms. Since the C.Y.O. sponsored inter-
school games in regular seasonal play-offs, St. Vincent's became one
of the teams involved in these games. Games with other schools
were played at St. Vincent's. But they were also played on other
school grounds. Therefore, the teams began to travel throughout
Marin County. When they reached the semi-final stage, they trav-
elled to Oakland, and in the finals, San Francisco became the scene
of their triumphs and losses. Fired with the enthusiasm so characteristic of him, Monsignor changed the uniform of the band to a
green and white ensemble, and brought the band along to many
C.Y.O. events. He also organized a drum corps independent of the
band. In the parades in which St. Vincent's boys now participated,
the green and white C.Y.O. flag was carried together with the stars
and stripes. A new life had been infused into the school and a
highly organized athletic program became part of its very life.

It was in the same year, 1935, that another generous benefactor,
the De Laviaga's gave one of St. Vincent's most valuable posses-
sions, its beautiful $12,000 outdoor swimming pool. Constructed
of tile, with two divisions, one a small pool for the little ones, and
the other a regulation pool with diving board, this beautiful orna-
ment to the plant was located on the site of Father McKinnon's
building, at the east end of the two long wings. Surrounded by the
beautiful gardens on the west side, the grotto of Lourdes at the
north, the play yard on the east, and the school building on the
south, it occupies the center of the area where the boys live and
play. Opened on Ascension Thursday, May 10, 1934, it has been
another source of health, of skill, and of training. Many St. Vincent's graduates have won athletic trophies in later years because
of the skill they acquired in St. Vincent's pool. This pool became
the center for annual swimming events. Various organizations are

Lourdes Grotto, erected to the memory of Monsignor McElroy's parents.

The new Administration Building, front view.

The new Administration Building, view from rear garden.

always needed to sponsor the trophies and medals awarded on these occasions.

But athletics was not to be the only healthy outlet for the boundless energy of his boys. The talent for showmanship in Monsignor McElroy has already been pointed out. Now it was to be used to benefit the boys and the school. Since Christmas, 1922, the Ignatian Council of the Young Men's Institute, known as the Y.M.I., had come to St. Vincent's for a Christmas party when candy and gifts were distributed to the boys by the members. Monsignor McElroy felt that it was also proper that the boys should entertain their guests. He began, therefore, a series of annual Christmas shows sponsored by the boys. The choir performed dressed in their choir dress. Plays were given and pageants portrayed. The Sisters sewed for day on the costumes designed by the Monsignor. The boys practiced and drilled until perfection was reached. Many a boy achieved legitimate success and felt pride in a job well done for the first time in his life through the medium of these shows. Such entertainments were not limited to Christmas time in Monsignor McElroy's administration. Each year, his name day, the feast of St. Francis de Sales on January 29, and St. Patrick's Day, were always occasions for at least a small program. The silver jubilee of his ordination on June 21, 1935, was the occasion of a fine entertainment.

Present at this entertainment was St. Vincent's new assistant, Father William Burke. Monsignor McElroy had to be out quite frequently because of his C.Y.O. activities and Father Weber was kept busy on the farm. Besides, of late, the senior assistant had not been feeling well. This second assistant therefore was sent on June 19, 1935 to aid Monsignor McElroy, who immediately felt that Father Burke could do the most good by teaching in the school. This happy appointment was to effect another internal change at St. Vincent's. Following many hours of discussion among these priests, it was decided that the commercial high school program be abolished and that the high school boys of St. Vincent's be given an opportunity, open to high school boys everywhere, of receiving a college preparatory education with instruction in the arts and sciences necessary for admission to the colleges of the state. This certainly was a change of major proportions. If Father Lootens or Mr. Mullany, if Brother Xenophen or Father Crowley could have been present, what a change they would have found in this. No more "farming out at fourteen". St. Vincent's boys graduating from college. Why not? But it took the faith of Monsignor McElroy in his boys and the courage of Father Burke to make the first beginnings in this enterprise.

The new two year academic high school began in August, 1935. Latin, algebra, geometry, history, English, and religion formed the solid foundations of its curriculum. That this was a step in the right direction has been fully demonstrated by those who have graduated from college in the past fifteen years. U.S.F., St. Mary's, Santa Clara, and Annapolis have been the scenes of higher education for some twelve of St. Vincent's boys. U.S.F. has graduated Dr. Angelo Leoni of Petaluma, Capt. John Hunt, U.S.A., Francis Maher, Neal Sweeney, and Joseph Buzzo. St. Mary's graduated George Farnham; and Santa Clara has been the scene of education of one of the best known, Bill Bruce, together with Dawson Wright, Murray Ackerman, and Joseph Stowers (1956). Greatest pride is taken in Ensign Chris Brown, U.S.N., who graduated from Annapolis in 1954. Were it not for this momentous decision taken in 1935, these boys and others whose names are unknown to us, would not have been able to achieve their educational success because they would have lacked the background and the incentive to aspire to college.

St. Vincent's received a scare on August 25, 1936, when Monsignor McElroy suffered a heart attack. As he was taken to St. Mary's Hospital in San Francisco, prayers began to storm heaven that he would live and be able to enjoy the fruit of his labors for a few years at least. He lived, but it was not until October 16, 1936, that he was able to return. From that day on, he had to live a much curtailed life. Remaining a great deal in his rooms, he directed operations from the priests' house where he said his Mass and had most of his meals. His labors had definitely shaken his health very badly.

The year 1937 was marked by the second visit of Archbishop Mitty[20], who on May 26, 1937, confirmed eighty-one boys, the largest number confirmed at St. Vincent's in several years. Three weeks later, on June 15, 1937, was held the Silver Jubilee celebration of the ordination of Father Weber. Five days later, on June 20, 1937, the first retreat at St. Vincent's for the Sisters was held, conducted by Father Albert Casey, S.J. This priest was to prove to be another faithful friend of St. Vincent's. For over twenty years he has come on the eve of the First Friday to assist in hearing the boys' confessions. In the same year, in the fall, the first retreat for the boys was conducted by Father Cornelius Murray. This first retreat marked the beginning of a new spiritual program for the boys. Monsignor McElroy had reacted against the old program that he had found on taking over the administration of St. Vincent's. At that time and for many years previous, assistance at daily Mass had been a regular part of the program. Monsignor McElroy realized that good habits of religion must be based on personal conviction and personal habits, not on routine group habits or regimentation. Therefore, he had eliminated the daily Mass from the program. Now with Father Weber and Father Burke available, a morning Mass was celebrated in the main chapel which was optional for the older boys. Therefore their attendance was of their own volition. Any habit of attending became a personal habit and had depth and meaning. This custom has been preserved to the present day. Confessions were heard on Saturday night during definite times. The boys were free to go as they wished. Monsignor McElroy was bringing the boys' life at St. Vincent's closer and closer to home life.

Three years of the academic high school program had manifested a need for more practical subjects for boys who had little inclination or ability for such studies as Latin or algebra. The need for manual training, both as a school subject and as an outside activity, was felt more and more. To meet this need, in 1939, Monsignor McElroy built two large shops close to the school-dining room building. On April 22, 1939, Archbishop Mitty arrived and gave Confirmation to eighty-eight boys and then blessed the new shops. This same year was marked by the termination of Sister Hedwig's term of office as Superior and the appointment of Sister Henrietta.

One of the biggest days in the life of St. Vincent's occurred on October 14, 1939. It was St. Vincent's Day at Treasure Island. Since the World's Fair was in full progress, the members of the Ignatian Council of the Y.M.I. felt that all St. Vincent's boys should see it. They chartered six Greyhound busses which left St. Vincent's at seven A.M. All the grades below the sixth were divided among sixteen Sisters, each with eleven boys to chaperone for the day. The men teachers and prefects had the boys above the sixth grade. Under police escort, the excited caravan reached Treasure Island. There each group had a guide to conduct them around the Fair, each guide a member of the Ignatian Council. All day long the three hundred twenty-five boys roamed the vast spaces of the Fair grounds. That night at eight-twenty the six busses drove up the lane to St. Vincent's with their loads of tired but happy boys, accompanied by very tired Sisters and instructors. Two months later, the boys expressed their thanks by means of the seventeenth annual Christmas show.

Monsignor McElroy had for several years hoped for a final building, but it was not until 1940 that he was able to realize his plans. In that year, due to several legacies received, he was able to build the gymnasium. This building was located in the little boys' yard, parallel to the 1912 building. It contained a full size basketball court, a large shower room, and locker room, and upstairs, a large meeting room. Serviced by its own heating plant, the gym turned out to be a life saver on rainy days and in cold weather. It was to have a great deal to do with the production of winning teams. The dedication date was set for May 28, 1940. The Drum Corps was on hand, dressed in their green and white uniforms. Acting as an escort, they led the procession to the lower yard. They were followed by the thirty-eight boys who were to receive Confirmation after the dedication, all dressed in spotless white. The vested choir formed the third group, The six smallest boys formed the honor guard for the American flag which, after it was blessed by Archbishop Mitty, was hoisted to the new flag pole atop the gymnasium.

These years of triumph and of accomplishment were now to be followed by three years marked by sorrow. The first event occurred on November 23, 1940. It was Saturday night. When nine o'clock struck, both Monsignor McElroy and Father Burke wondered why Father Weber had not come to the house. They knew his habits were as regular as a clock. Fifteen minutes later, Monsignor began to get nervous. Eventually Father Burke went to the administration building. The light was on in Father Weber's office. Thinking he was working later than usual, Father Burke returned to the house. But some time later, there was still no sign of Father Weber. Returning to the administration building, Father Burke looked in the window. Father Weber was seated at his desk. A knock brought no response. After some effort, Father Burke got into the office. Father Weber had his Breviary in his hand, open to the office of the day. He had died as he had lived, in prayer and alone. The loss of this devoted priest was very hard on Monsignor

McElroy. For eighteen years they had worked together. In grateful memory of his co-worker, Monsignor erected a crucifixion group in the midst of the fields that had been the scene of Father Weber's labors. The statuary was dedicated on the anniversary date of the burial of Father Weber, November 27, 1941.

Ten days later was the tragedy of Pearl Harbor, which had definite effects on St. Vincent's. Her alumni would now be involved in the armed forces. Monsignor McElroy would find new cause for grief. The annual Christmas show was suspended on account of the war. St. Vincent's now became a center of activity because of its proximity to Hamilton Field. Air raid shelters were arranged for the boys. Steps were taken to black out the place at night. Anti-aircraft installations were set up in the fields. An air of tension sat upon the Monsignor.

On August 18, 1942, St. Vincent's had received the twentieth Sister, the sixth among the teaching Sisters. On December 1, 1942, the number was reduced to nineteen by the death of one of the most faithful and beloved, Sister Coletta. She had been the infirmarian since January, 1929, a service of thirteen years. She had a heart attack on Thanksgiving Day, was taken to St. Joseph's Hospital in San Francisco on November 29, and died on December 1, 1942, at the age of seventy-five. Four months later St. Vincent's received word that one of its alumni, Bill Bruce, beloved by Monsignor McElroy, had been killed in the service.

These events were to prove too strenuous for the health of the Monsignor. On January 27, 1943, he himself had a slight stroke but he was back home by February 10, 1943. For the next few months he had to be extremely careful, but by Easter Sunday, April 25, he felt well enough to sing the High Mass in the morning. That afternoon he was driven to San Francisco where he had dinner with his sister and brother. He was home and in bed early, but at ten P.M. another heart attack came upon him. Within a few minutes he was dead. St. Vincent's was an orphan again, having lost its second father.

The boys sang a Requiem Mass for their beloved Father on Tuesday, April 27. Father Burke was the celebrant and Bishop Connolly, Auxiliary Bishop of San Francisco, presided. The body was then transferred to St. Mary's Cathedral where the funeral was held on Wednesday, April 28. In the funeral sermon, Father Powelson, Monsignor's successor at the Working Boys' Club, summed up his work at St. Vincent's:

> *"From an orphanage he converted an institution into a home in which he was the father, the Dominican Sisters the mothers.*
>
> *From an orphanage, he pioneered the cottage system wherein he was the elder brother of the family.*
>
> *From an orphanage he established a school, of the graduates of which he always spoke proudly, followed their careers closely, shared their joys gladly, shouldered their sorrows intimately."*

St. Vincent's stands today, a monument to this priest whose genius made it a model institution of its kind.

The Band in 1950.

Chapter XX

ROUNDING OUT A CENTURY
1943 - 1951

Two months after the death of Monsignor McElroy, Archbishop Mitty appointed the new Director. History repeated itself. Just as Father Birmingham, the assistant Director, had succeeded Father Lootens in 1868, so now Father Burke was appointed to succeed Monsignor McElroy.

Born in Galbally, County Limerick, Ireland, on September 23, 1907, the son of Cornelius and Julia Burke, he received his elementary and secondary education in the local schools. In 1924, he entered St. Patrick's Seminary at Thurles in Ireland. Four years later, he came to the United States, and entering St. Patrick's Seminary, Menlo Park in September, 1928, he pursued his theological studies there until his ordination on June 20, 1931. Father Burke was then assigned to St. Leo's Church in San Jose where he served as assistant pastor until 1935. On June 19, 1935, he was assigned as assistant to Monsignor McElroy.

After seven years at St. Vincent's, working closely with the Director, Father Burke was excellently prepared to succeed the Monsignor. He knew his mind, his methods, and was therefore prepared to carry on the same regime. From the date of his appointment as Director, June 20, 1943, until the end of the year he was alone at St. Vincent's. Finally, on December 30, 1943, Archbishop Mitty appointed Father John T. Dwyer as the assistant. There began a partnership between these two priests which, if not of as long duration as that of Monsignor McElroy and Father Weber, was nevertheless, as close. In July, 1944, Father Dwyer was appointed principal of the school succeeding Father Burke, who now devoted himself to the problems of administration. One month later, on August 17, 1944, Sister Henrietta's term as Superior expired. Her place was taken by Sister Marie Therese, O.P.

Christmas Day in 1944 found a situation very new in the life of St. Vincent's. After the usual Christmas dinner at noon, Father Burke sent the remaining forty or fifty boys into San Rafael to the show. During the afternoon, there were no boys at St. Vincent's. Certainly this was the first time in history that all the boys were out on Christmas Day. This fact shows that the change of policy made by Monsignor McElroy was producing its own results. The dependent boys of 1944 were not abandoned as were the boys of 1884. With a start made at Christmas, it now became a policy to try to get every boy out of St. Vincent's, not only on such occasions as Thanksgiving, Christmas, and Easter, but also during part of the summer vacation. In the summer of 1946 contacts were made with various summer camps and arrangements completed so that every boy who was not taken by relatives for part of the summer would at least have a two weeks' vacation away from the normal school year environment. This policy has continued to the present time.

One of the first projects of Father Burke's administration was the completion of several years of work inaugurated by him as principal of the school. With the approval of Monsignor McElroy one of the rooms in the school building had been beautifully finished in panelled wood with fluorescent lighting for a library. Books numbering several thousand volumes had also been gathered. But the change in administration came before this new library could be catalogued and put into regular use. In the fall of 1945, Father Burke saw his dream come true. The Dominican Sisters loaned one of their gifted members, Sister Carmelita, who spent four months in the laborious work of cataloging St. Vincent's library. The work was finally completed by her and other Sisters in 1946. St. Vincent's now had an excellent library in addition to its many other valuable training programs.

These years, 1944 and 1945 saw improvements also in the external administration. It had been fourteen years since Monsignor McElroy had completed the building of St. Vincent's. Even the newest building, however, needs careful watching and gradual replacements as parts begin to wear out. Many of the things accomplished by the new Director were of such a nature, unseen yet necessary replacements. For example, the job of renewing the mattresses for 330 beds was a huge and expensive task. It was a far cry from the kind of mattress and renewing job done by Sister Mary Paul in 1888. Yet it had to be done. Also the buildings were beginning to show their age. The newness was wearing off. Therefore, Father Burke began a program of repainting a certain number of buildings each year until the whole institution was repainted every five years.

Perhaps his biggest contribution, certainly the most expensive one, was the renewal of the heating system and especially the installation of hot water. Just as Father Crowley in 1894 had finally solved the water problem which had increased as St. Vincent's had expanded, so now Father Burke solved a similar problem in regard to heat. What happened at St. Vincent's happens frequently. A heating plant is set up for an original set of buildings. Then an additional building is erected and attached to the present heating plant. Later another building goes up and it too is hooked into the same boiler. Eventually the task imposed on the original boiler becomes an impossibility. St. Vincent's found, for example, that when heat was needed in the auditorium, some two city blocks from the power house, all other heat had to be shut down to get the pressure great enough to reach the auditorium. Therefore in the spring of 1945, a new boiler was ordered capable of sufficient pressure to take care of all St. Vincent's needs. It was an exciting day in July when the railroad flat car was shuttled into St. Vincent's siding and slowly edged to the side of the boiler room. Probably that was the last time a train came up the siding tracks to St. Vincent's. The installation commenced. Now a second and most important matter was remedied. For the first time, hot water was made available in the living units. The boys of the 1920's and 1930's had washed in cold water as did their predecessors of the 1880's. Only in the showers had there been hot water. Now every faucet in every house gave forth an abundance of hot water. St. Vincent's no longer was in the same class as the cold water flats of New York.

Such projects as the mattress renewal, the painting of the buildings, and the installation of the new heating system were expensive. It was to the credit of Father Burke that he was able to put the institution on a sound financial basis. After all, the generous benefactions obtained by Monsignor McElroy had ceased. St. Vincent's now had to maintain itself. Two means of solidifying the finances were found, one on the farm and the other in the Community Chest. With the death of Father Weber the management of the farm had been given to Mr. Thomas Ducey. The tradition established by Father Weber was continued. It was during the war years that the farm was most appreciated. When families were living on rations, when red stamps had to be doled out for meat supplies, St. Vincent's lacked neither beef, nor pork, nor fowl. The second source of sound financial backing was found in the Community Chest of San Francisco. St. Vincent's had been a charter member when the Chest was established in October, 1922. During these war years the Chest assumed more and more of the deficit until its annual grant exceeded $40,000, which is about one-fifth of the total operating expenses. By careful living within a given budget, and the supplementary aid given by the San Francisco and Marin County Chests, St. Vincent's is able to maintain itself from year to year.

The Second World War had other effects on St. Vincent's which were not so beneficial. For one thing, the manpower shortage hit St. Vincent's very badly. The Prefects for the older boys and the teachers in the upper grades were nearly all younger men. Some were called into the service. Others were simply tempted by the wages available which far outstripped teachers' salaries everywhere. The full impact of the situation hit St. Vincent's in 1946. Two prefects and three teachers left at one time. Replacements were extremely difficult to get, and for some weeks the situation was tense. This same year, 1946, the beloved Sister Sebastian who had been privileged to occupy the first new building, died at Mission San Jose after a short illness. In August, Sister Maximiliana had been sent to replace Sister Sebastian. But on Thanksgiving Day, November 28, 1946, she also died. These difficulties made 1946 a memorable year for the administration.

But there was a bright side to the year also. In internal matters, St. Vincent's made progress. A survey was made that year by Father James O'Shea of Catholic Social Service in San Francisco in fulfillment of the requirements for his Master's Degree at the University of California. The purpose of the survey was to determine whether St. Vincent's was fulfilling its avowed purpose of being a home for dependent boys. The study revealed that it was definitely fulfilling its purpose in life.

There were 335 boys at St. Vincent's that year, its top capacity, reached because of the war. One hundred and sixty-four of the boys had entered St. Vincent's from the public schools, one hundred and two from parochial schools. The remaining fifty-nine had started at St. Vincent's in the first grade. The children were divided among the grades as follows:

1st grade: 43	4th grade: 48	7th grade: 31
2nd grade: 46	5th grade: 39	8th grade: 27
3rd grade: 48	6th grade: 33	9th grade: 14
		10th grade: 6

Perhaps the most interesting table compiled by Father O'Shea was that which showed the length of stay:

Year of Entry	Number of Boys Still in the School
1945	68
1944	69
1943	64
1942	75
1941	40
1940	16
1939	18
1938	8
1937	3
1936	—
1935	4
	335

There is a very noticeable drop after a stay of four years. The writer appended the following note concerning the four who had been in St. Vincent's since 1935: "The four in the institution since 1935 are brothers—full orphans with no relatives. One attempt to place them together in a foster home failed and they asked to be returned to St. Vincent's."

"With only three unqualified boys out of three hundred thirty-five there doesn't seem to be any complaint to be found with the carrying out of the institution's intake policy. So, in every way, St. Vincent's is fulfilling its purpose. It cares for dependent boys and for them alone. As it has carried out the letter of its founders' wishes, it carries out the spirit also. The various Directors have struggled to keep its physical standards of the highest. At present it is completely equipped and beautifully appointed. It affords its boys the best of care, a splendid education, and the group living which has been adjudged necessary for their wellbeing."

What was not mentioned in the survey was the program of leisure time activities which had been developed and which is so important in the lives of the boys. About this time, Father Burke organized a "Hobby Shop" which he put under the care of Mr.

Mark Harting, one of the faithful Prefects. Originally located in one of Monsignor McElroy's shops, it is located today in the gym. Approximately fifty boys are members at all times, each one working on model planes, model ships, and other crafts which are available today for boys. At about the same time, a troop of Boy Scouts was organized under the care of Mr. James Quigley, who is currently the athletic coach. Four patrols were maintained for several years. These thirty-two boys were completely outfitted and took active part in the Marin County scout affairs. Most valuable of all their activities was the acquiring of a camp site at Tamarancho, the Marin County scout camp. The unimproved area staked out by St. Vincent's boys was improved during the spring and summer months and for several years prizes were captured for the best camp site.

Marin County has always abounded in animals. Just as these attracted Don Timoteo Murphy to Marin's shores over one hundred years ago, so animals have attracted St. Vincent's boys over the years. In 1943 a Saturday hike program had been inaugurated. On Saturday afternoon either a priest or a prefect took some forty boys for a hike through the beautiful hill country of Marin County. These hikes developed until smaller groups of boys began to go on their own hikes. It was this latter group that began to discover animal tracks, bones, and furs. Letters were written to magazine advertisers of fur trapping societies. Slowly, as is the way with boys, a club was formed. Racoons, weasels, skunks and other animals were trapped. Some were retained as pets, others were used for the pelts which the club members learned to cure.

In the fall of 1946, Father Burke requested that the annual Christmas show be revived. The war had stopped the Y.M.I. from their annual visit, but even though they, nor the Knights of Columbus who had also come on several occasions, were not involved, the show was to be presented for the families and friends of the boys. Needless to say, its chief value would be in giving so many boys an opportunity to excel in the show. The director for these occasions was Father Dwyer who aimed to get as many boys involved in the show as possible. The choir, which always presented several selections, numbered about sixty boys. The band of thirty boys, under the capable direction of Mr. Russell Johnson of San Anselmo, worked for weeks to present several numbers. The first grade, third, or fourth grade offered group recitations or pantomimes. A play involved several boys and the Christmas pageant at the end required a large number. On one such occasion 200 of the boys were involved in the entire Christmas show. The Sisters commenced again the tremendous work of costuming these many boys. The choir cassocks and surplices had to be fitted, cleaned, and ironed. The band wore the immaculate white pants and green and gold jacket. The members of the cast were all costumed according to their character parts. Staging, ushering, parking, program distribution, all these details were cared for by older boys. The Christmas show had again come to be part of the life of St. Vincent's. In 1947, the Call-Bulletin newspaper of San Francisco began furnishing a Christmas show and valuable gifts to St. Vincent's boys. This has continued for several years.

The leisure time activities of the high school boys received special consideration because of their age. Although they were involved in all the activities mentioned, they had some of their own. Saturday afternoon found them in San Rafael, sometimes at a show, sometimes skating. Since 1944 they had been members of the Federation of Catholic High Schools. This involved attendance at meetings at other schools every six weeks. It also meant an opportunity to attend dances. With the opening of the school year several kind lay people came in to teach the boys to dance. Ursuline High School in Santa Rosa always included St. Vincent's boys in their dance invitations. In later years dances have also been held at St. Vincent's.

From this outline it should be quite clear that a St. Vincent's boy certainly has opportunities for occupying his leisure time well. He can participate in a highly organized athletic program; or he can join the hobby shop, the trappers, the scouts, the band, or the hikers.

The year, 1947, was a memorable year in the life of St. Vincent's. On June 12, 1947, came the joyous news that Father Burke had been named a Monsignor. Recognition of St. Vincent's and its Director by the Holy Father had been accomplished a second time. On August 3, 1947, St. Vincent's received a new Sister Superior in the person of Sister Angela Marie. This Sister was to witness several members of her community celebrate the Silver Anniversary of their arrival at St. Vincent's. On September 1, 1947, Sister Simplicia completed twenty-five years of service to the boys of St. Vincent's. On September 2, 1949, Sister Loyola and Sister

Rt. Rev. William M. Burke, Fourteenth Director of St. Vincent's—1943-1950.

The Swimming Pool—dedicated May 10, 1934.

The Gymnasium—dedicated May 28, 1940.

Leopolda also completed twenty-five years. Three days later recognition was given to the fact that Dr. Leo Boyle had devoted a like period of time to the dental care of the boys. In his devotion during all those years, he was assisted first by the late Sister Coletta, and then by her successor for many years, Sister Camilla. In their own quiet way these devoted people have served the boys well.

It was on May 3, 1950, that the Monsignor Burke-Father Dwyer combination was first broken. On that night while returning from the school to the house, Father Dwyer fell and fractured his hip. His place in the school was taken by St. Vincent's second assistant, Father Aloysius Sullivan, a graduate of the School of Social Science of the Catholic University of America, who had been appointed on November 10, 1949. He now took over the school for the remainder of the semester. When Father Dwyer returned on August 15, 1950, there was also a new Sister Superior in the person of Sister Verona.

The month of January, 1951 brought surprising news to all St. Vincent's. Reminiscent of 1888, St. Vincent's lost both its Director and its Principal at the same time. Monsignor Burke was appointed Pastor of St. Catherine's Church in Martinez, California, and Father Dwyer was appointed assistant at St. FinnBarr's Church in San Francisco. Father Sullivan remained as Assistant Director and the new Principal of the school. The transfer took place on January 17, 1951.

CONCLUSION

The fifteenth in the succession of Directors was Father Clement McKenna. He brought to his new post a love of boys and a valuable background. Born in Oakland, California on May 9, 1911, the son of Michael and Anne McKenna, he received his elementary education at St. Joseph's School in Berkeley. He entered St. Joseph's College, Mountain View, in September, 1925, where he spent six years. In September, 1931, he began his studies at St. Patrick's Seminary in Menlo Park. Ordained a priest on May 22, 1937, he served as an assistant for a few months at St. Brendan's in San Francisco. In September, 1937, he received his first acquaintance with Marin County by his transfer to St. Anselm's Church in San Anselmo, the scene of his labors for the next four years. His appointment to Holy Cross Church, San Francisco, lasted for less than two years, for on March 1, 1948, Father McKenna followed the example of Father McKinnon in 1898 by volunteering for Chaplain service in the U. S Army Air Force. On his return from military service in May, 1946, he was appointed to St. Patrick's Church in San Francisco, the post he held at the time of his appointment as Director of St. Vincent's on January 17, 1951.

The four and a half years of Father McKenna's administration have been marked by two accomplishments. The first was a gradual increase in staff. Mr. Raymond J. Hebel, graduate of the Loyola University School of Social Work and formerly with the Catholic Home Bureau of Chicago, Illinois, came to St. Vincent's in July, 1951. Since that time he has headed the Social Service department and has taken the responsibility for the in-service training of prefects. The present roster of lay faculty composed of prefects and teachers is as follows, given in the order of seniority. Among the prefects, Mr. Mark Harting who has devoted fourteen years to St. Vincent's is in charge of the Hobby Shop. Mr. James Quigley, seven years on the staff, was made Director of athletics in 1952. Mr. Joseph Devaney, and Mr. Timothy Bell are the other Prefects. Most recently a grammar school coach and part time remedial teacher for the Junior High group was obtained in the person of Mr. Gormon Herminghaus.

In the school several changes have occurred since Father Sullivan became the Principal. In September, 1952, the teachers were

Rt. Rev. Clement J. McKenna, Present Director of St. Vincent's.

relieved of any prefect work. One year later a fourth lay teacher was added so that the ninth and tenth grades would be completely separated in all classes, a cycle course having been formerly used in some subjects. In the past few years the high school has grown so that in 1954 there were forty boys in that group. Spanish was substituted for Latin as a subject. The classrooms were completely refinished in the Junior High and High School department. The lay faculty consists of Mr. Frank Schofatal, teaching at St. Vincent's since 1950, now in charge of the tenth grade and organizer of an excellent choir among the older boys; Mr. Charles Carmona in the ninth grade; Mr. Thomas Bushore in the eighth; and Mr. Edward Morin in the seventh grade.

In addition to these ten lay workers there are four other trained lay personnel working for the good of St. Vincent's. These include Dr. Leo Boyle the dentist, and Dr. Joseph Hawkins, M.D., who with the exception of the war years, has been the school doctor since June, 1933. The school nurse is Mrs. Julia Holland who has been at St. Vincent's since she replaced Sister Camilla in November, 1952. She is capably assisted by four local part-time nurses. The present band master is Mr. Charles Brewer.

The religious staff, besides the two priests includes nineteen Sisters. Sister Rosalia has been the Superior since August, 1953. The housemothers for the boys from the first through the sixth grades are: Sisters Wunibalda, Guala, Mauritia, Simplicia, Thecla, and Gerarda, the last having given over twenty years of service at St. Vincent's. The Sisters teach in the school from the first through the sixth grade. These include Sisters Rosalia, Josephine, Bertrand, Antonia, Jordan and Consolata. Sister Loyola, for the past few years has devoted herself to remedial work with small groups of boys from the third to the sixth grades. For thirty-two years she had also served as sacristan in the chapel. The kitchen department is under the care of Sister Marka and Sister Walburga, and the dining rooms under Sister Gertruda, whose service totals eleven years, and Sister Angelina. Sister Manessa, who has been twenty years at St. Vincent's, and Sister Florentina take care of the boys' clothing. In addition to these tasks of teaching, being housemothers, cooking, sewing and laundry work, it would be difficult to describe the multitude of duties quietly and efficiently performed by these devoted Sisters for the past thirty-three years.

After the retirement in September, 1953, of Mr. Thomas Ducey, the management of the farm was entrusted to an alumnus of St. Vincent's, Mr. George Caesari. With the help of seven others, including John Barron, another alumnus who has charge of the chicken ranch, Mr. Caesari supervises the cultivation and care of some 1200 acres, the milking of fifty cows, the breeding, grazing, and slaughtering of 110 steers, 150 hogs and an average of 2,000 chickens. Nine more are employed as watchman, engineers, carpenter, baker, and kitchen help. The office is staffed by Mrs. Maureen Wernecke who has been the bookkeeper since 1925 and the secretary is now Mrs. Maureen Hunter. The late Mrs. Hazel Whelan served in that capacity for over twenty years until her fatal illness enforced retirement.

Besides surrounding himself with this capable staff of fifty-five people, Father McKenna's second accomplishment has been the erection of a final building to the magnificent plant. In January, 1954, construction started on a new grammar school. Located between the rear of the gymnasium and the south end of the dining room building, it has formed the third side to the small boys' play yard. Designed by architect Erneste Winkler and built by Mosher Brothers of Corte Madera the new school containing six grades and a room for remedial work, was occupied in October, 1954. It will be dedicated on May 22, 1955, the date of the centennial celebration.

Once again, in recognition of St. Vincent's outstanding work and of his own contribution to the welfare of the institution, the Director was named a Monsignor by Pope Pius XII on December 6, 1954. Under the care of Monsignor McKenna, Father Sullivan and the Dominican Sisters nearly 300 boys are presently finding a home, an education, and character training as well as emotional stability at St. Vincent's through the excellent program maintained there. As the institution commences the second century of its existence, it should no longer be an orphan. It has found its place as a leader among child-care homes.

NOTES AND BIOGRAPHIC SUPPLEMENTS

1. Sister Frances McEnnis continued to serve God and community at the girls' orphanage in San Francisco until her death on January 18, 1879.

2. Sister Corsina McKay returned to the Market Street Orphanage for another year; in 1857, she was transferred to the Sisters Infirmary at Los Angeles and in 1861 to St. Joseph Seminary also in Los Angeles. She died at St. Joseph's Central House, Emmittsburg, Maryland on September 22, 1888.

3. Edward Muybridge was born in Kingston-on-Thames in England in the year 1830. He came to the United States when he was twenty-one, and traveled to California as a commercial photographer employed by the commercial photographic firm of Bradley and Rulofson as a photographer of outside orders and was known as the "outside view man" of the firm. In October, 1873 he selected Marin County as the scene of his labors. His arrival in San Rafael received the following notice in the *Marin Journal:*
   "Mr. Muybridge, the justly celebrated photographer is in town with his camera. He intends to take a view of the beautiful town of San Rafael. He will also photograph Mt. Tamalpais. Mr. Muybridge is located at the galleries of Bradley and Rulofson, corner of Montgomery and Sacramento Streets, where you can sit down to go up stairs."
   The photo of St. Vincent's was taken during the week of October 19, 1873, and was made into a stereoptican postcard from which the picture in this book was made. Mr. Muybridge left California in 1881 and went to Europe. A few years later he returned to the United States, confining his work to Pennsylvania and other eastern states.

4. Father Robert Maurice served as Pastor of Stockton until October 6, 1860 on which date the Archbishop transferred him to St. Francis Church on Vallejo Street. Three weeks later on October 24, because of the untimely death on October 9, 1860, of Father Daniel Slattery of Marysville, Father Maurice was appointed Pastor of Marysville. On February 3, 1861, the new Bishop, Most Rev. Eugene O'Connell, was consecrated in Ireland as Vicar Apostolic of Marysville. He left for California at once and arrived in San Francisco on April 24, 1861. Meanwhile many of the priests who had been serving in what was now the new vicariate left their posts before the arrival of the new Bishop and returned to their native countries leaving Bishop O'Connell with only six priests to begin his work. Among those who left was Father Maurice who evidently returned to England, leaving Marysville on April 30, 1861.

5. Father Louis Auger remained as Pastor of Sonora for seven years. He served the mining country of Tuolumne and Mariposa Counties. During those years Sonora had a population of about 2,500 people. Father Auger had not only a fine church but also a flourishing school with over 100 children. On November 20, 1867, the Archbishop transferred Father Auger to Suisun, as the first resident Pastor. He remained here until 1872. What became of him then we have no record, but it is assumed, since it was customary, that he returned to his native France.
   It is interesting to note that in Sonora, Father Auger succeeded Father Lootens; whereas at St. Vincent's Father Lootens succeded Father Auger. In other words they simply exchanged places.

6. Bishop Lootens found life in Idaho extremely difficult. He had only three priests under him to aid him in administering to the needs of the many Indian settlements committed to his care. Finally after eight years of such labors, broken in health, Bishop Lootens resigned his See on July 16, 1876. He returned to Vancouver Island. where he had worked before coming to San Francisco, and there lived in retirement until his death on January 13, 1898.

7. Father Birmingham remained as acting Pastor of St. Joseph's Church until October 5, 1877 when the Archbishop transferred him to St. Patrick's on Mission Street. On September 22, 1879, he was appointed Pastor of Sutter Creek in Amador County. After almost four years in the Mother Lode country, he was transferred to St. Matthews in San Mateo. On June 6, 1885, he became Pastor of St. Brigid's in San Francisco. On Thursday, August 29, 1889, he went on a visit to see his friend, Father Michael Riordan, Pastor of Menlo Park. On Saturday afternoon while conversing with Father Riordan, Father Birmingham suffered a stroke, fell unconscious, rallied for a short time, received the last sacraments and about 6:30 P.M. died. He was only fifty years of age.

8. William S. O'Brien was one of the Silver Kings, a member of the famous Fair, Flood, Mackay and O'Brien team. These became millionaires through their speculations in the Virginia City Comstock Lode of the 1870's. William O'Brien was born in Dublin in 1826 and brought to New York as a child. As a youth he worked in a New York grocery store. He arrived with the gold rush crowd in San Francisco on July 6, 1849. He entered a number of partnerships one after the other. In 1856 he joined forces with James C. Flood in a saloon. From this the pair rose to dealing in silver stocks, ownership of bonanza mines, banking and real estate. O'Brien never married. He remained unspoiled by his immense wealth living rather moderately with simple tastes. When he died on May 2, 1878, his fortune amounted to twelve million dollars. He handsomely provided for his relatives and was most generous to charities.

9. Archbishop Alemany resigned his See on December 28, 1884. He returned to his native Spain where he died on April 14, 1888.

10. Father Lagan remained as Pastor of San Rafael until 1899 when he was transferred as Pastor of Sacred Heart Church, San Francisco. He held this post until his death on Christmas Eve, 1904.

11. Archbishop Patrick W. Riordan succeeded to the See of San Francisco on December 28, 1884, after having served for one year as Coadjutor Archbishop.

12. Father McKinnon was Pastor of Rio Vista from 1893 until 1897, when he was succeeded by his own brother, Father Bernard McKinnon. In May, 1898, the Spanish-American War was at its height and Father McKinnon volunteered as Chaplain of the San Francisco Regiment of the National Guard and was accepted by his personal friend, Colonel James F. Smith. He was sent to Manila and there in August, 1898, he performed an act of bravery which helped to end the war and save Manila. Across the "no-man's land" which separated the two armies he went alone to visit the Archbishop of Manila and the Commanding General, carrying the peace terms offered by the Americans. A few days later, on August 13, Manila was captured with small resistance. Father McKinnon remained in Manila with the Army of Occupation and was made Superintendent of Public Schools and Cemeteries. He came home for a brief visit in August, 1899. Returning to Manila he remained there until his death on September 24, 1902. His body was brought home and San Francisco gave him a hero's funeral. In grateful remembrance for his bravery a statue was cast and erected in Golden Gate Park. It stands on the main drive between Sixth and Eighth Avenues.

13. Father Crowley returned to the Youths Directory on September 22, 1894. On July 23, 1899 the cornerstone was laid for a new Directory on Nineteenth and Angelica Streets. The old Howard Street building he gave to the Little Sisters of the Poor. The building on Nineteenth Street was destroyed by the 1906 fire. The third Directory was then built on Church Street overlooking Mission Park. Later Father Crowley purchased a farm at Rutherford, Napa County, where he organized St. Joseph's Agricultural Institute. Father Crowley died on February 2, 1928.

14. Brother Michael remained as Director of the Berkeley Academy until September 6, 1910 when he was appointed bookkeeper of St. Mary's College in Oakland. He was stricken again with serious illness on June 10, 1911, when he was taken to St. Mary's Hospital, San Francisco. There he died on September 28, 1911, after suffering very severe pain.

15. Brother Xenophon was Visitor of the San Francisco District for six years. Afterwards he became Director of St. Joseph's Academy in Berkeley. In 1919 he was sent to Sacred Heart College in San Francisco. There, ten years later, he was stricken ill in the Chapel on August 19, 1929 and died a few minutes later.

16. Brother Paul was in charge of Holy Cross School in Santa Cruz for four years. Then in 1919 he again succeeded Brother Xenophon, this time as Director of St. Joseph's Academy in Berkeley. On August 3, 1925 he became Treasurer of the San Francisco District with his residence at Sacred Heart College in San Francisco. In 1931 he was moved to St. Mary's College High School in Berkeley as Prefect, but he lived only one year, dying there on December 29, 1931.

17. Brother Peter remained as bookkeeper of St. Mary's College until his death. He moved with St. Mary's from Oakland when it occupied the new buildings at Moraga in 1928. There he died on May 24, 1933.

18. Archbishop Edward J. Hanna was sent as Auxiliary Bishop in 1912. He succeeded as Archbishop on July 1, 1915. Due to advanced years and poor health he resigned on March 21, 1935. Retiring to Rome, he died there on July 10, 1944.

19. Brother Vellesian was Director of the Christian Brothers School in Sacramento until June, 1925, when he was transferred to the new St. Mary's College on August 15, 1928 and was placed in charge of purchasing for the kitchen. In 1936 he took charge of the office at St. Mary's High School in Berkeley, and in 1940 he held the same office in Sacramento. On August 15, 1942, he returned to St. Mary's College High School and remained there until his death on April 28, 1950.

20. Archbishop John J. Mitty was appointed Coadjutor Archbishop of San Francisco on January 29, 1932. He succeeded as Archbishop on March 2, 1935.

CHART I

Name	Date of Admission	Age on Admission	Age on Departure	Date of Departure	Place To:
Edward Thomas	Jan. 6, '77	9	14	Jan. 6, '82	To Mr. Wynne, San Jose
William Dunbar	Jun. 17, '77	9	14	Jun. 15, '82	To a grocery in San Francisco
Richard Hoare	May 3, '79	10	13	Feb. 5, '82	Taken by his sister
George Cusick	Apr. 3, '79	7	8	Feb. 14, '82	R.I.P. in Orphan's Cemetery
Robert Hamilton	Nov. 10, '81	11	12	May 12, '82	Taken by Father Walsh, Sacramento
Edward Blaney	Jan. 22, '72	10	20	May 31, '82	Went to Galveston
Thomas Gough	Oct. 26, '75	8	15	Feb. 15, '82	Sent to Druggist Selzer, Oakland
John Quinlan	Mar. 16, '76	9	15	Jan. 25, '82	Taken by Father McEvoy for a rancher
James Sweetman	Apr. 19, '73	7	16	May 14, '82	To Harvard College, Boston
John Forde	Dec. 28, '74	9	17	Apr. 15, '82	To Mrs. Murphy, Petaluma

CHART II

Name	Date of Admission	Age on Admission	Age on Departure	Date of Departure	Place To:
Joseph Vincent	Dec. 16, '68	3	18	Jul. 4, '83	Left voluntarily
William Shannessy	Aug. 13, '72	5	16	Feb. 7, '83	To San Andreas
Daniel Gaffney	Mar. 22, '73	6	15	Oct. 6, '82	To San Pablo
Thomas Silver	Sept. 20, '78	11	15	Aug. 1, '82	To priest in Santa Rosa
George Sullivan	Mar. 13, '79	12	15	Oct. 8, '82	Took French leave
Frank Moore	Apr. 22, '79	12	16	Jul. 6, '83	To North Beach
Albert Costa	Dec. 15, '79	13	17	Nov. 17, '83	To Mr. O'Neill, Martinez
Edward Barrett	Jun. 14, '76	9	15	Dec. 30, '82	To Healdsburg
Michael McDonald	Sept. 30, '76	9	16	Apr. 3, '83	With his father
James Callan	Mar. 12, '77	10	15	Jul. 1, '82	To his mother in Napa
Matthew Nunan	May 6, '77	11	21	Still at St. Vincent's on Dec. 31, 1887	
John Shehan	May 19, '77	10	16	Jun. 1, '83	To a ranch in Petaluma
John Fitzgerald	Jun. 27, '79	13	18	1882	In laundry
James McCarthy	Jul. 20, '80	13	16	Jul. 15, '83	To mother in San Francisco
Charles Decleer	May 7, '81	15	17	Oct. 7, '83	With father in Oakland

With the departure of Father Croke in 1888 there is no more record kept of boys over age fourteen. Therefore, it is impossible to tell what eventually became of Matthew Nunan.

CPSIA information can be obtained at www.ICGtesting.com
Printed in the USA
LVOW081718290212

271003LV00006B/126/P

9 781462 053780